PENGUIN BOOKS

LOCAL HEROES

'In many ways the Loch Fyne buyout represents the polar opposite of the fast-buck, quick get-out model of private equity buccaneers, the scale of whose avarice is matched only by the mountain of misery they leave in their wake . . . How sweet must be the upside: working in a community and working for the community. Working for a team whose values you share and respect' *Herald*

'As business books go it is in a class of its own . . . A rip-roaring yarn with the absolute minimum of financial jargon and always lucidly explained' *The Oldie*

'Honest, inspiring, uplifting and, above all, a good read' *Insider Magazine*

'An extraordinary story of personal commitment and vision which led to commercial success and community achievement. Employee ownership works' Sir Menzies Campbell

'Compelling and inspiring, this is a book about global heroes – people who see the future first and make it happen' Sandy Balfour, Chair, Divine Chocolate

'David Erdal has taken us to a story of ordinary people creating a company out of the mists of Scotland for the benefit of all the employees. Loch Fyne Oysters is a fabulous business success yet it is as far away from city slickers and fat-cats as you can possibly get. Read it and realise that there is "another way"' Andy Law, author of *Open Minds*

'An interesting and valuable account of employee-owned business based on hard-won experience. There is also much to be learned from this book that is applicable to more conventional business managers' Sir George Mathewson, Royal Bank of Scotland

David Erdal studied Chinese at Oxford, then worked as a teacher in Mao's China. After gaining an MBA at Harvard, he returned to Scotland and led the family paper mill, Tullis Russell, into all-employee ownership. In 1989 he won the Scottish Business Achievement Award. After obtaining a Ph.D. at St Andrews on the psychology of sharing, he went on to be MD of Baxi Partnership, which structures and funds all-employee buyouts of medium-sized companies. He lives in St Andrews.

Local Heroes

*How Loch Fyne Oysters Embraced
Employee Ownership and Business Success*

DAVID ERDAL

PENGUIN BOOKS

PENGUIN BOOKS

Published by the Penguin Group
Penguin Books Ltd, 80 Strand, London WC2R ORL, England
Penguin Group (USA) Inc., 375 Hudson Street, New York, New York 10014, USA
Penguin Group (Canada), 90 Eglinton Avenue East, Suite 700, Toronto, Ontario, Canada M4P 2Y3
(a division of Pearson Penguin Canada Inc.)
Penguin Ireland, 25 St Stephen's Green, Dublin 2, Ireland
(a division of Penguin Books Ltd)
Penguin Group (Australia), 250 Camberwell Road, Camberwell, Victoria 3124, Australia
(a division of Pearson Australia Group Pty Ltd)
Penguin Books India Pvt Ltd, 11 Community Centre, Panchsheel Park, New Delhi – 110 017, India
Penguin Group (NZ), 67 Apollo Drive, Rosedale, North Shore 0632, New Zealand
(a division of Pearson New Zealand Ltd)
Penguin Books (South Africa) (Pty) Ltd, 24 Sturdee Avenue, Rosebank, Johannesburg 2196, South Africa

Penguin Books Ltd, Registered Offices: 80 Strand, London WC2R ORL, England

www.penguin.com

First published by Viking 2008
Published in Penguin Books 2009
1

Copyright © David Erdal, 2008

The moral right of the author has been asserted

Typeset by Rowland Phototypesetting Ltd, Bury St Edmunds, Suffolk
Printed in Great Britain by Clays Ltd, St Ives plc

A CIP catalogue record for this book is available from the British Library

ISBN: 978-0-141-03560-4

www.greenpenguin.co.uk

Penguin Books is committed to a sustainable future
for our business, our readers and our planet.
The book in your hands is made from paper
certified by the Forest Stewardship Council.

For
Philip Baxendale

The form of association, however, which if mankind continue to improve, must be expected in the end to predominate, is not that which can exist between a capitalist as chief, and workpeople without a voice in the management, but the association of the labourers themselves on terms of equality, collectively owning the capital with which they carry on their operations, and working under managers elected and removable by themselves.

John Stuart Mill
Principles of Political Economy

As for the future, your task is not to foresee it, but to enable it.

Antoine de Saint-Exupéry
Citadelle

Contents

PART TWO:
Making Employee-ownership Work

Introduction
Smiles at the Head of the Loch

Loch Fyne Oysters, a cluster of whitewashed buildings at the head of Loch Fyne, is a place where people smile a lot.

On the shore of Scotland's longest sea loch, deep among the glorious western mountains, it is a business that provides a wealth of healthy seafood, local produce, sustainable and pure. It is a place of pilgrimage, almost. Visitors travel huge distances for the food in the restaurant and the shop. They look through the glass panel at the people slicing salmon in the Clean Room. They sup shellfish soup as they gaze down the loch, which winds away west through the enclosing mountains towards the distant open sea. Since this is the west of Scotland, you can't always see the mountains for the surly low clouds and the driving rain. But on random days the sky is blue, the air is still, columns of smoke rise vertical from the chimneys of the cottages scattered round the loch, and the mountains are reflected perfectly in the mirror-surface of the water. At these times you can gaze at it all meal long without feeling the need to converse, and Loch Fyne Oysters becomes a place of meditation. It is hard to have mean feelings in a place like that, at a time like that.

Visitors tend to smile because they like the food and the view and the relaxed atmosphere. The employees smile because they own the place. They all have a stake in the business. It is theirs, and no one else's.

Smiling is not usually one of the measures tracked by managers, but there is no doubt that the smile count rises when the business is owned not by distant, wealthy, greedy shareholders but by all who work in it. They are in charge of their destiny and they love it.

On 4 April 2003 Loch Fyne Oysters was sold to all its employees. It didn't cost them a penny – the company itself financed the transfer into employee-ownership. Following the death of the company's joint founder and main shareholder, the much loved Johnny Noble, the company had been on sale for months. The suitors from outside included a vet, an ex-chicken breeder, a father-and-son fish-farming company and, the front runners – the most knowledgeable and congenial of the four – a large privately owned seafood-processing company based in the north of England. There was a serious risk that if they won they would move the operations to England, leaving just the Oyster Bar and the shop.

The employees – the only party not advised by a merchant bank – put in the highest bid: just under £4m. This caused frustration and consternation among the bidders and their backers. To the 112 employees, it brought sheer joy.

When one company buys another, the results are often disastrous. Even in purely economic terms, academics have shown repeatedly that acquisitions tend to destroy value.[1] They also tend to destroy people. Managers are sacked to make way for the acquirer's hit men, while employees are 'let go' to reduce costs so that the acquirer can attempt, often in vain, to recoup the cash spent on buying the company. Those who are lucky enough to retain their jobs – people who have spent years building up the business, identifying with it, making personal sacrifices far beyond the demands of their contracts – often see their ideals betrayed, their hopes for the company and for themselves dashed. Many are demoralised, some immediately, and some only later, as the consequences become clear. The animating spirit of the company is often shattered.

An employee-buyout is different. In the early summer of 2003 large wooden signs were displayed prominently in the restaurant and the shop, carved with the words: 'Loch Fyne Oysters – a company owned and run by its employees'. From then on, the same slogan has been printed on every package of seafood dispatched from the head of Loch Fyne.

And since the employee-buyout, productivity in Loch Fyne Oysters has soared.

This book starts by delving into the building of the company, from its first stirrings in the mid-1970s through its founding in 1977, then the seven lean early years and the increasingly successful and confident expansion which followed in the further twenty years before the employees bought the company. Then it tells the story of the employee-buyout: why it was done, how it was done and how it has proved the foundation for continuing success. Employee-owners are different from ordinary employees – they are partners in the enterprise, and when they are treated as partners, they will go to extraordinary lengths to achieve success. But old habits, ideas and attitudes carry over from the past in everyone, manager, waitress and fish filleter alike. The book finishes with a description of the early steps taken in Loch Fyne Oysters to make the partnership feel real to everyone involved – and some of the bumps along the way.

The story is full of heroism, the heroism of ordinary people as well as the two extraordinary men who founded the company. It gives pointers to others who may wish to go down this path. Any company can do the same. Employees can almost never afford the cash to buy the company that employs them. But an employee-buyout in the form used by Loch Fyne Oysters, financed not with employee money but using a trust funded by the company, can be achieved by almost any company, of any size, in any business. Any company can switch to being owned by all its employees, paying a fair market price to the previous owners, and without the employees putting up the money. And it can stay employee-owned for as long as the business can be kept successful – which is usually a lot longer than an equivalent company owned by outside shareholders. It sounds too good to be true. But it works.

It was my good fortune to run the Baxi Partnership fund that provided the structure and about half the funding for the Loch Fyne Oysters employee-buyout. At the time of writing the fund has supported eight companies: six employee-buyouts, one employee-owned start-up and one company that was already employee-owned. For some, business has been tough, and at least two of them, now profitable and growing, believe that without employee-ownership they would no longer be in existence. Others, like Loch Fyne Oysters, have commented on the customer interest: many people prefer dealing with a company that will share its profits among the whole community of employees rather than passing it into the hands of distant, already wealthy owners, with the fat-cat managers taking a cut on the way for services rendered to the owner, not to the customers or the employees who actually make the company successful. It is just common sense that people will work harder and feel better about their own company than about someone else's.

I came to run the fund, and so to write this book, because in 1994 I led the all-employee buyout of Tullis Russell, a papermaking company owned by the family into which I was born. In the process I saw how people's lives can be changed when they move from being just employees to being employee-owners, together in charge of their company and so of their own future. I also saw how it led to a sustained improvement in the performance of the business.

Seeing this transformation in others changed me too: I caught the employee-ownership bug. There seems to be no cure for this, and the book is in part an attempt to spread the virus to others. Those who catch it may sleep less soundly, until as owners they sell their companies to the employees or as employees they buy the companies they work for. But they will have found a way to transform lives, including their own, entirely for the better.

In the twenty-first century we are utterly dependent on people organised in businesses. They provide us with what we need to live and also with what we want. Without them we would struggle, naked and starving, without possessions, without technology, without education, without medicine, without government. The dream of doing these things through state-ownership and control has fallen away, and we are left with businesses and markets dominating the world we live in.

The building of a new business is one of the great creative acts of our time, making something that people want where there was nothing before. Not just that: creating a business is creating an institution, a process that gives people what they want again and again and again, capable of running from the present into the distant future. This book starts with the story of how Loch Fyne Oysters was created, the inspirational energy and dedication that turned the barren head of the loch into a renowned centre for healthy and sustainable seafood. The company had unlikely beginnings, with bizarre and marvellous characters, people whose story invites sympathy and wonder and laughter and admiration. Like many tales of creative acts, the story of the invention and building of Loch Fyne Oysters is about people driven by strange compulsions, stretched to their limits, clinging to the cliff by their fingernails, twisting and turning, often with no idea what to do next, boggle-eyed at calamities, sleepless with fear, rescued by wholly unexpected strokes of luck, cheerfully risking everything, winning when it seemed impossible, plunged into the depths, collapsing with exhaustion, sharing whisky round the fire in the evening, arguing a lot, laughing like banshees and loving what they were building. And in the process coming to love one another, without ever saying so.

A business is at bottom a community of people – everyone who works for it. And within the community, a business distributes two things that have caused more violent deaths than anything else in history: power and money. One of the background themes of this book is the distribution of those twin drivers – who gets to make decisions and who gets to share in the wealth that people create in businesses. Another is the ideology embodied in conventional wisdom, which keeps the privileged rich and powerful, and the people acquiescent. In the foreground are two things: the excitement of building a business, and the way that employee-ownership restores people to their humanity, giving them understanding and influence and wealth. Employee-ownership is a quiet revolution, not one that concentrates power and wealth into the hands of the greedy, but one that redesigns the company to distribute understanding and influence and wealth widely. People in such companies tend to build strong, productive businesses.

Employee-ownership works. It is more productive and spreads wealth more widely than capitalism or socialism ever did, and it gives people the opportunity to live their working lives more fully than has ever seemed possible under any system.

No wonder the smile count rises.

PART ONE

The Story of Loch Fyne Oysters before the Buyout

No bird soars too high, if he soars with his own wings.

William Blake
The Marriage of Heaven and Hell

1. Two Desperate Men: the Laird and the Fish Man

The idea that became Loch Fyne Oysters was born out of the desperation of two men, Johnny Noble and Andy Lane.

In 1977, these two radically different people both lived near the head of Loch Fyne, though they had yet to meet. They had things in common that they could easily talk about – a love for the glorious hills and the loch, the wildness of the place, the closeness to nature, a respect for people with practical skills. Another preoccupation they shared would transform their lives, and the lives of many people around Loch Fyne and beyond – a deep and increasingly desperate drive to find livelihoods for themselves and their dependants. Johnny Noble's dependants were numerous, though mainly unrelated to him, and Andy Lane's were simply a dream, a virtual future family.

Everyone who met Johnny Noble was impressed by one thing in particular: his extraordinary temperament. Scientists tell us that temperament is highly heritable, that is to say, it is shaped to a great extent by genes. Whatever the impact of our experiences growing up, for which we can also often thank or blame our parents, our underlying character seems to be largely a given at birth.

The people who passed down their genes to Johnny Noble already showed their potential. His grandfather, Sir Andrew Noble, made a fortune equipping the British

navy with the first rifled barrels for its huge guns, the
guns that helped win the First World War. In 1905 Sir
Andrew invested part of this fortune in buying the Ardkinglas estate, several thousand acres at the head of Loch
Fyne, thereby achieving a very British form of success: a
move out of 'trade' to become landed gentry. Sir Robert
Lorimer, Scotland's most fashionable architect at the time,
designed for him in stone a grand estate house overlooking the loch. Sir Andrew's cellar book shows that he
would spend more on a case of sherry than on a year's
pay for a shepherd on his estate. When he died, his son
John, Johnny's father, used his legacy simply to live on
the estate as a landed gent. He married Elizabeth Lucas,
who came from a family that also seemed blessed with
character-forming genes: she was such a richly warm
and welcoming individual that her husband lived somewhat in her shadow. Elizabeth's brother, Harry Lucas,
was a co-founder of Warburg's, a respected merchant
bank in London.

These streams from the gene-pool combined in Johnny
to create an unstoppable, lovable, roguish, hilarious character; his parents then gave him an upbringing that made
him a gentleman, without ever corralling or dampening
this temperament.

Andy Lane came from the opposite end of the country
and of the social scale. In his own words:

My forebears were just very humble farm labourers, salt-
of-the-earth country people, and we used to work on
the farms. My aunt worked in service, as did a lot of my
great-aunts. I had a great-uncle who was a blacksmith.
And these are people I remember with huge affection.

When Andy Lane speaks of affection, he speaks simply. He knows what he feels, and he tells you.

Neither Johnny Noble nor Andy Lane could properly be described as a normal child. Johnny Noble was an only son in a grand house dominated by large numbers of female relatives. His character shone through from the beginning, gregarious and in demand with family, schoolfriends and villagers alike. On one occasion as children, his two sisters, with a couple of cousins, were performing a ballet for the adults on the lawn in front of the great estate house. Their brother suddenly appeared, wrapped in a long cloak scavenged from an attic. He charged on to the lawn to join in the ballet, and with dramatic panache threw back his cloak to disclose his body, completely naked. All his life he was to make grand entrances, and all his life whole gatherings would, like this one, burst into laughter at his antics. Without Johnny Noble's flair, Loch Fyne Oysters would not have flourished as it has.

At that time, before the Second World War, boys born into wealthy British families rarely escaped a boarding-school education. Few nations in the world have taken naturally to the idea that at the age of seven or eight boys should be separated for most of the year from their families, in order to live with, and be educated among, boys of similar backgrounds. The idea had taken hold in Britain in the nineteenth century. The purpose was partly to 'stiffen the backbone', to prepare young men for ruling the Empire, for living far across the world in sometimes very tough conditions, governing the uncivilised natives but remaining ramrod-straight themselves, no matter how isolated and lonely they were. That was the theory, anyway. By the 1940s the Empire was on its last legs, but the notion of boarding school was now deeply ingrained, and Johnny Noble was sent to Eton.

Of all the public schools, Eton has the highest social cachet. The polish gained by boarding there has a special quality to it, an extra awareness of superiority, an outward confidence. After Eton Johnny Noble could hold his own in any company. But perhaps because he was fending for himself as a boarder from such an early age, he seems to have learned to guard his inner life closely. Everyone was his friend, and he was a hilarious showman-friend to all, but personal, intimate information he kept to himself. Nevertheless, he had from Eton a set of friends who remained loyal all his life, and who were to prove crucial to him in many ways, not least in clubbing together to give him the means on one occasion to avert serious disaster and on another to achieve real success.

Boarding-school friends have an easy way with one another. When they meet up they can usually slot back together with jocular familiarity, and they often support one another faithfully. But every boy at boarding school experienced his own pain, and one way to deal with it was to turn viciously on any weakling who showed his in public. So from a young age the cost of boarding was often a lack of ability to express tender emotion, perhaps even to experience the more vulnerable feelings that were so dangerous to expose. Hence stems, perhaps, one root of the famous British reserve. Johnny Noble may have learned from this, even while he loved being at Eton. In later life, at the same time as being a magnificent host, a charismatic companion and a great performer on social occasions, he always seemed curiously shy. Old friends muse on this, puzzled still.

He never married, was never seen with a girlfriend, gave no public sign of a love life at all. When he talked, which he did well, often in a loud voice, he would man-oeuvre carefully around combinations of sibilants that might trigger his stutter – perhaps the only outward sign of a buried inner life.

After school, like so many of his ilk, Johnny Noble went to Oxford, then had a spell in the army, in the Argyll and Sutherland (he called them the Agile and Suffering) Highlanders, after which he joined Warburg's, the family merchant bank. Thus far, his career showed no sign of anything unusual. There were thousands of boys with his privileged background who took similar paths.

As a boy among his country relatives Andy Lane knew that he was loved, but his boyhood passed in less flamboyantly sociable surroundings than Johnny Noble's, and he was more of a loner.

When he was two years old, his brother was seven and his sister nine. His sister contracted polio and, with terrible suddenness, died. Their father never recovered. Pictures disappeared from the walls; years later he would still weep at certain songs; he could not bear to visit his young nieces, whom Andy loved. It was the 1950s, and grief was not a public affair, even within the family. For the young boy growing up, his father's moods created a puzzle that he was left to work out for himself.

One summer, at the age of eight – the age at which Johnny Noble was dispatched to boarding school – Andy

Lane had an experience that would shape his whole life, and ultimately inspire him to shape the lives of many other people too.

A little country road went past our home. On the other side was what we always called the 'brickfield'. There was an ancient brickworks in it, disused and overgrown. There were diggings, there was water, there were trees. It was a beautiful, beautiful place. A few cattle used to graze there. I remember going up there as a small boy, being amongst the trees, by this water, very overgrown, very green, very dense, almost tropical – and just getting this absolute sense of oneness.

He pauses.

It was not something that I was looking for, not something I was trying to summon up or anything. It just happened.

Another pause.

And to a little unformed eight-year-old it was very comforting. I don't know how long I was there, in this kind of thrall. Then, in my tiny, childlike way, I made this absolute vow: I was going to protect nature, protect wild things.

All of this is spoken simply, directly, naturally. This vow is made in such a way that there can be no doubting it, but there is no emotional charge. It is too real for doubt, too deep for histrionics. He is just telling the facts.

Even then I probably felt the threat, because you could see farming changing and old pastures being ploughed up. It was a big 'I'm going to do this in my life' kind of thing. It was very strong, and it has come back throughout my life.

As his unusual life unfolds, this experience is the key to understanding it. His is a life dedicated above all to protecting wild things, protecting nature. Not for any advantage or any ideology – he is the opposite of a fanatic – but because he experienced it at the deepest level as simply the right thing, perhaps the only thing, to do. At the age of eight he found his place in nature.

Finding his place in society was not so easy. Social life in his native village of Oundle, in the shadow of a seventeenth-century public school, suffered from withering overtones of condescension and snobbery. His father, brought up in his grandparents' tiny alehouse, had left school at fourteen, sweated through correspondence courses to become an accountant, and ended up chairman of the local council. His mother worked indefatigably for numberless charities. Always bright, Andy Lane won a scholarship to the local 'direct-grant' (part-privately funded) school. His family could never have afforded the fees. Laxton school was then absorbed into Oundle, one of the public schools. Like Eton, it was filled with boarders, the children of rich people separated from their families.

It was an eye-opener, going to a public school and seeing the feet of clay of people that my aunt and great-aunts, the domestic servants, would have thought of as their betters. Seeing it clearly. And seeing that they had really none of the rich – generalizing horribly because these are all human beings – none of the rich humanity of the unpretentious country people that were round me in my early upbringing.

There would have been gentle, loving boys, no doubt, at this school as any other. And, as at Johnny Noble's school, they would have learned to suppress any such feelings, and join in the struggle. However, Andy Lane had the advantage of going home every night.

He got to university, the first of his family to do so, and chose to study English literature, inspired by visions of wandering in nature like Wordsworth. Soon realising that the subject was unlikely to provide him with a livelihood, he switched to biology, specialising in marine biology. A few months after graduation he jumped at the chance to head into the wilds of western Scotland to work on a salmon farm. In those early days it was possible to believe that salmon farming would save the wild salmon. Andy Lane believed this fervently, seized by a mission to save these beautiful wild creatures in nature.

One thing these two very different people had in common was that neither could find a place in which to settle happily. Johnny Noble left Oxford after just one year, without a degree, and Warburg's after only a little longer – he said he could not even begin to work out what he was supposed to do there. He was also constitutionally incapable of fitting in with the dress conventions of the banking fraternity – to the horror of the sombre City gents who ran the bank, he would wear slip-on shoes with his superbly tailored suits.

Staying in London, he then worked in the wine trade, starting his own business after some years. Moving among people like himself, in a world that gave him free rein to be as he was, he discovered a talent – he proved to be a superb and instinctive marketer. Not only could he sell, he could leave his imprint for ever in the memories of people he dealt with, usually suffused with affection. A meeting with Johnny Noble had a certain intensity. A large part of this was his ability to make you feel that you were the most interesting person he had ever met, and throughout his life he would be hailed by people who considered him a close friend because of a single encounter years earlier. The fact that often he himself would have forgotten them was incidental. Wherever he went he would wear a black Scottish tam-o'-shanter, a bonnet retained from his army days, and he continued wearing it for the rest of his life, replacing it with a similar one when it was stolen. He may have had the traditional upbringing of a toff, but he was very far from being conventional. Johnny Noble was finding his own path.

Encouraged by his mother, who taught him to appreciate other people for their characters and not for whether they had a good education or fancy clothes, he held a deep respect for people who did practical things with skilful hands. He had spent time with them in his childhood on the estate, the stonemasons and gamekeepers and deerstalkers and carpenters, people whose characters and activities had shown him a strong contrast with the refinements of his schooling. He himself was clumsy. He would wave his hands apologetically: 'I'm not very good with me dabs,' he would say, failing the simplest test of dexterity, and at the same time passing the charm test with ease.

He went to France and sought out small vineyards, run by people like the Ardkinglas estate workers, people who did the work themselves, without affectation, producing superb wines in the process. These were the wines he imported, and their unique quality was soon recognised. His first sales in London were naturally to his many friends, some of them quite discerning customers. His wine business began to grow and at last Johnny Noble had his own income.

In 1972 his father died. There is no telling what feelings Johnny Noble experienced at that death, which was to transform his life. As the only son he inherited the Ardkinglas estate with its glorious house at the head of the loch. But it turned out that his father had been borrowing heavily against the estate, and with it came huge debts, greatly increased by inheritance tax, which had not been planned against. Johnny Noble also inherited the outgoings. There were estate workers to pay, but little or no income to pay them with. He felt the responsibility keenly. *Noblesse oblige* really meant something to him, as it had done to his parents: as the laird of the estate he had to find income for the estate workers. So, typically employing the most unexpected and apparently unsuitable person – an ex-ship-builder – as the estate manager, he set about various projects designed to do that: starting a sawmill to make fence posts, a garden-furniture manufacturing business and others. None of them worked. The debts got worse.

Meanwhile Andy Lane, a few years Johnny Noble's junior, working on the salmon farm, found himself living with his dog in a rickety old caravan on the southern shore of Loch Fyne, dreaming of finding a cottage and a wife and settling down to a simple way of life in tune with nature. Of course, living by Loch Fyne was wonderful. Working with fish, spending much of his time in the open, fixing up tanks and pipework for the fresh water to flow over the salmon eggs, watching them hatch, the springing to life of new creatures, elegant and graceful and so vibrantly alive – all this was deeply enjoyable. And he had a job.

He had been delighted to get this job, and not just because of his hope that it would help to save the wild salmon. It would also let him stand on his own feet, with an income of his own. He hoped that what people said about having a job was true: it would connect him to other people, give him a role in life, be fulfilling. He knew that the long-term unemployed were subject to loss of self-esteem, depression, abuse of drugs and alcohol, marriage breakdown. Having a job would make life a thousand times better. For a brief moment, at the beginning, he felt that optimism. It would engage him as an autonomous human being, and empower him.

But it didn't.

The only autonomy left once he had taken the job was the ability to leave, to give it up again. It was true that he had some money at the end of the week, which allowed him to survive, and in this fairly small company he quickly got to know everyone and was treated pretty decently. But the small company was owned by a bigger one, which was owned by a bigger one again. Locally, there wasn't a feeling of 'them and us'; it was mainly 'us'. 'They' were the people in the bigger companies that owned the small company that employed 'us'. If he asked questions, they answered as best they could, but it was clear that nobody knew much except about the immediate operations. To questions about the company itself – how were they doing, what were the long-term plans? – there seemed to be no answers. Wanting to make the contribution that he knew he was capable of, Andy Lane made suggestions about how things could be improved: they were generally ignored. After a time, he knew that he was establishing a hatchery which, when successful (and it was looking good), would save the company money as well as providing a more secure supply of young salmon. He knew that he personally would not share in the profit this created, though he still felt proud of a job well done. Increasingly, however, he experienced unease at the great corporate structure above them that had the power to make all the big decisions, to direct what they did, and to suck away the money they made. It seemed like a cold hand gripping his heart, and he began to feel the urge to get free of it. If he stayed too long he might succumb, and never be free.

He wondered whether this was the consequence of having a manager he didn't get on with, or whether there was something about the nature of having a job, of working for a company, that meant that this would always be so. Tentatively, he concluded that it was just the way things were in companies. His direct manager could have been more open, and certainly didn't need to criticise work that they both knew was perfectly satisfactory, just to show who was boss. But no matter what happened, at bottom that would not change things – Andy Lane saw that ultimate control lay in the distant corporate structure above them, and he felt more and more uncomfortable. It seemed that neither he nor, he realised in a minor epiphany, his manager, had any real influence.

Quite apart from his relationship with the company and its servant, his boss, Andy Lane was also beginning to realise that the salmon-farming methods used – the crammed cages allowing the parasites to multiply, and the ferocious chemicals used to try to control them – were increasingly polluting the environment. Far from saving the wild salmon, this was becoming a serious threat to them.

With this developing understanding, Andy Lane no longer felt lucky to have his job. He even found himself wondering if it was sensible to work as hard as he was doing. Once the hatchery was set up and stable, they might not need to keep him employed. He realised with some disappointment that if the company could save money by getting rid of him and employing an unskilled person, just out of school maybe, then it would probably do so. In this frame of mind, when he was grading the salmon, the fish had a knack of slipping out of his hands into the overflow pipe into the loch, to freedom. The protest was secret, but satisfying nonetheless.

He also realised that his wages gave him little hope of ever attracting a serious girlfriend, let alone of settling down to bring up a family, the dream that often filled his quiet moments. A wife, children, a cottage by the loch, a simple life together . . .

Although it was wonderful to be living in the wild and wacky west, as Andy Lane thought of it, and although there were times of sheer joy in the hills and along the shores of the loch, conditions were not great for attracting a mate. The caravan was ramshackle, with a leaking, plastic roof-hatch that blew off in storms. Once, over a period of months, he woke up to a headache every morning. Then, one quiet evening as he was cooking on the tiny gas stove, he heard a hissing sound and discovered that a gas pipe had not been properly sealed. Every time he used the stove it was filling the caravan with gas. The fact that he had not been poisoned or blown up owed less to good fortune perhaps than to the fact that the caravan was so pitifully draughty.

This narrow escape crystallised his thinking: he had to get out. Might he not find a way to work for himself? It seemed impossible, but the idea settled at the back of his mind.

Ideas themselves are not enough to change anything: for a new idea to have a meaningful impact, there has to be a real psychological drive behind it. In this case the drive was there long before the new idea appeared. It is often like that. First the crisis builds, and only when it is at breaking point does the idea appear, resolving it. Otherwise the idea simply floats into the mind, into a conversation or a daydream, and floats away again into oblivion, or perhaps recurs as no more than an occasional fantasy.

These two men, Johnny Noble and Andy Lane, still strangers to each other, stalked around the head of Loch Fyne, primed to burst into creative activity. With this level of internal pressure, anything could trigger an explosive new beginning.

2. The Idea: Oysters in the Tide

Living in his decrepit and dangerous caravan, working for a pittance on the salmon farm, Andy Lane was a young man with normal instincts. He very much wanted a social life, one involving people of his age, with chat and laughter, and ideally a girlfriend too. He was tall, rangy, slim, dark-haired, with something of a bird of prey about him. As a student he had enjoyed some success, socially and romantically, so he felt reasonably confident. His relationships, however, had proved turbulent. At times he wanted rather desperately to form one that would last.

At Cairndow, the village at the head of the loch, the pub was the centre of much of the social life in the village. This went some way towards providing companionship, though there were few people of Andy Lane's own age, and very few women, none of them available.

He was earning an extra £6 a week – a sum worth having in 1977 – as a diver at the fish farm, collecting the dead salmon from the bottom of the cages, and he earned some more by diving to collect scallops and to check moorings for boat owners along the coast. With this extra money he managed to keep up an old banger of a car, and so at weekends he began to explore other pubs and hotels in the area. Eventually he came upon Ardfern.

Ardfern is a yachting centre, a village with a marina set in the shelter of another sea loch, Loch Craignish. It is a stopover point for yachtsmen heading to or from the sailing Mecca of Mull, Skye and the Outer Hebrides, and, for some who don't do much sailing but like to have a boat anyway, to display their success to others and to themselves. Ardfern lies not far from one of the great tidal phenomena in the world, the Corryvreckan race with its huge, roaring overfalls, but is well sheltered from the south-westerly storms that regularly pound the coast. You can get a shower and a hot meal there, precious commodities when you have been weathering the seas and winds. In addition to the yacht owners, Ardfern attracts all kinds of people: experienced sailors and novices, crew members and engineers and the like, many of them exactly the sort of youngsters that Andy Lane wanted to spend his spare time with. And most of them were ready to have a chat and a laugh.

The Galley of Lorne pub usually had a sprinkling of women of all ages, some, like most of the men, much inclined to drink, some really attractive. Andy Lane, in his hormonal state, found almost all of them attractive. He had no illusions about being able to win them on equal terms with the yachtsmen, whose pockets seemed to overflow with money. But the atmosphere was stimulating, filled with bursts of loud laughter, slightly louche, as if an orgy might be just about to break out. He went there frequently, to sit and chat with people over a long-drawn-out pint and to luxuriate in the sensual atmosphere. Compared to the regulars in the pub back at Cairndow they seemed cosmopolitan, adventurous, varied, not much troubled by convention. Promising.

Everyone in the pub at Ardfern enjoyed the wildness of the west, as Andy Lane did. Some, like him, had settled there. One Saturday he fell into conversation with someone he had seen around a few times, a man in his thirties. He often appeared with two others, one of them quite startling to look at, with long hair and a distant look in his eyes. But this night he was alone.

It turned out that the three men had started rearing oysters further up the coast. They had set up an oyster-bed well below the low-tide mark, and they dived for them. From the sound of it, things were not going too well. Their main diver, the man with the distant look in his eyes, was spending a great deal of time under water but it seemed there was little to show for it.

After a while, the man offered Andy Lane a smoke. It soon became clear that what was on offer was not conventional tobacco. History is vague on whether Andy Lane accepted or not, and, if he did, whether or not he inhaled, but he remained interested in the oyster venture and kept up with the three men at the pub from time to time. He decided that the distant look was the result of what he called the wacky baccy. The diver particularly enjoyed smoking a joint before he dived. His companions never seemed to make a connection between the smoking and the lack of productivity under water. The diver spoke with feeling about how lovely it was, just hanging under water, floating weightless in space, rising and falling gently with the change in buoyancy as he breathed, giving out streams of silver bubbles that rose lazily towards the surface, gleaming and wobbling with a life of their own.

In the end, the three ran out of money. Apart from their easy-going approach, one problem was that the oysters didn't grow too well. Andy Lane thought he might know why. In the wild, oysters tend to cluster naturally around the low-tide mark, not in deep water. If he were doing it, he would try putting bags of oysters where they would have an airing each time the tide went out. At first it was an idle thought, but then the idea took hold, and he would ponder it as he worked at the salmon farm. Then it clicked. *This was the kind of thing that might let him work for himself.* He could do it. He could be like them – in charge of his own life, and able to spend a lot of time in the pub at Ardfern. If it worked, he would have money, and he knew how to make it work. Thank God he had switched from English to marine biology.

But the tales of how difficult the oysters had been to market also stayed with him. And he recognised the hard fact that to start with, probably for a long time, there would be no cash at all, as every penny would be spent on building the business. So he did nothing about it. But the pressure inside had found a possible escape route. Maybe he could become an oyster farmer.

One autumn day in 1975, when Andy Lane was working at the salmon hatchery, a man appeared. Not very tall and quite stocky, he was wearing a faded, well-used canvas smock and a black bonnet with a bobble on top. Andy Lane thought he looked like an artist. He had seen him a few times and knew that he was the laird, that he owned the land on which Andy Lane had been building the hatchery by the shore. The gossip in the pub was laced with stories of his escapades – everyone seemed to like him.

Still some distance away, the man called a greeting, waving in a diffident, slightly awkward way. He had a rich, well-bred sort of voice, without sounding hugely confident.

Andy Lane responded.

The man didn't say anything else, and Andy Lane felt the need to fill the silence.

'The salmon hatchery's coming on.'

'Yes, I saw you b-b-building the tanks. Looks like a pretty good job.' The man held out his hands and gave a short laugh. 'I'm not much good at that sort of thing.'

And the two started chatting about the fish and the village and the estate.

They met often after that, just casually round the hatchery. Johnny Noble was intrigued by Andy Lane's knowledge, and Andy Lane was attracted by the laird's energy, humour and patent goodwill. He was also flattered by his open admiration of the work he was doing.

The two looked forward to their meetings. They exchanged stories of the wine business and the diving and before long they were trading a bag of scallops for a bottle of Gros Plant, one of the excellent wines that Johnny Noble had discovered. Soon they were doing the trade and then opening the wine and drinking it together by the fire in the billiard room in Ardkinglas House. This meant that a bag of scallops was being exchanged for only *half* a bottle of wine – but often the first bottle proved quite inadequate to the number of things they had to talk about, and so parity was restored by consuming a second. Johnny Noble called white wine 'pop' and drank it as if it were non-alcoholic. Perhaps for him it was, since he didn't seem to show the effects.

He sometimes talked about the cattle in the valleys and the sheep on the hills, bemoaning the prices. These hills were among the least-favoured agricultural areas in the whole of Britain. If you let a sheep loose in Romney

Marsh in England, when you brought it in again it would have doubled its weight. If you did that here, all you would find would probably be a dead animal, skin and bones, picked over by the hooded crows. Andy Lane suggested looking to the sea, which here in the west of Scotland was one of the most favoured areas in the whole of Europe. It was crazy that British tourists were going out to Spain in huge numbers and coming back raving about the wonderful seafood there. Most of the scallops, prawns, crabs and lobsters and a lot of the fish they ate in Spain was actually Scottish in origin. But the only seafood to be seen in Scotland was battered haddock from the east coast, sold frozen to fish-and-chip shops. If the locals would only realise the quality of Scottish seafood, it might become recognised as among the best in Europe. Since the transport would be minimal, the quality would be even better than in Spain. To his delight, Andy found ready interest from Johnny Noble, though neither of them saw it as something they might actually do.

One evening Andy Lane mentioned his thoughts about growing oysters. There were oyster shells all around the coast of Loch Fyne, but no oyster-beds any more. Johnny Noble sat up. During the war, when he was just a boy, he had been sent to collect oyster shells from the beach and grind them up to put grit in the feed for the hens. The idea of growing them hit him like an explosion in the brain. It was not just the childhood memory, it was the fact that the people he had dealt with through his wine business, the people in the London circles he moved in, old friends from school and others like them, all enjoyed oysters, preferably accompanied by a fine dry white wine which he would be happy to supply too.

Oysters had cachet, excitement. They were a challenge to eat; they made some people shrink away, but anyone who was anyone ate oysters, if only for show. Oysters brought a touch of pizzazz to a meal and perhaps to the diners' love life afterwards. They were the ideal dish for a show-off, and Johnny Noble's London circle was full of show-offs.

He agreed readily to the suggestion of doing a feasibility study. It sounded grand, a feasibility study, and Andy Lane smiled inwardly at his unaccustomed pretension. In his gut he knew that it would work. He would make it work. Perhaps they would do it together.

Neither of them slept that night. The conversation twisted and turned in their brains, filling them with energy and hopes and budding determination. The idea took root.

3. The Start: Dreams and Disasters

When you do something new, you're on your own. Most people who create new things suffer agonies along the way, and there are no guarantees at any stage. Many more fail than succeed.

The advice from all the business schools is that before embarking on a major project you must draw up a business plan. You have to think out every step and put numbers on it – how much it will cost, how much money will come in, and when. The discipline really is useful: putting the idea into numbers and dates shows clearly the great gulfs that you have to cross but have not yet thought through, and the gaps in the information available. A feasibility study is a business plan with an extra-high level of uncertainty – an attempt to see if the business might possibly work, given a range of assumptions that may only be guesses.

Andy Lane had never done a plan quite like this before. He realised how little they both knew, with the result that the plan, no matter how detailed, would be worth about as much as a few squiggles on a cigarette paper. But he thought about nothing else for days, and worked at it every evening until he had something to show.

Even for a feasibility study, there was an unusual level of uncertainty. For example, one of the important statistics that Andy Lane did not have was the mortality rate of farmed oysters. It would make quite a difference if 20 per cent died every year, as opposed to, say, 5 per cent. Plucking a random number from the air, he settled on 10 per cent. And one of the problems that he could not solve was the fact that seed oysters needed to grow in the sea for four years before they would be ready. How would an oyster farmer survive those first four years with no income? In the plan he put himself as still working for the salmon hatchery and Johnny Noble surviving he knew not how, but anyway with nobody other than the suppliers of oysters and transport being paid anything. In this at least he was prescient.

He talked to British Rail and found that they could send the oysters to London on the overnight train – and to anywhere else with a railway station too. This seemed a godsend: a perfect distribution system just 14 miles away, and not too expensive either.

Unsurprisingly, his projections showed that at the end of four years the business would be profitable. Then they would be able to pay themselves a salary.

Andy Lane was on tenterhooks when he handed the plan over to Johnny Noble. But the laird was in no mood to be sceptical. He had the bug too: for him, here was another way to provide work for the estate workers, and perhaps some income to bring down the debts at last. He had had a meeting with the Revenue recently; they had been polite, but very firm. He could pay the tax over some years, but pay he must. With his advantages he did not expect sympathy, and he thought he detected in the attitudes of the two officials a kind of ruthless satisfaction at his plight. His desperation was mounting, though he showed not a flicker of a sign that anything was other than perfectly fine. He mused to Andy Lane on the unsmiling pair with a job that did not allow them to be human, while in contrast the would-be entrepreneurs were undoubtedly human, and determined to stay so. They agreed to make a start.

The leap from idea to action is not an easy one. You can't get there by thinking – thinking will always block action, never trigger it. Then at some point the thinking ceases and something completely different comes into play. A switch is thrown and you just do it.

In this case, it was Andy Lane who made the leap. It was simple enough. Johnny Noble wrote a partnership agreement on less than one side of paper, they both signed it and they consumed a bottle of his champagne. Then Andy Lane worked his week's notice at the salmon farm, took the title of 'MD, Loch Fyne Oysters' and, since he had no money, went on the dole. The welfare state is accused of undermining entrepreneurship, but in the case of Loch Fyne Oysters there is no doubt that it fostered it, by keeping the twenty-six-year-old MD alive while the business was born. Which took a lot longer than the two men had anticipated.

On the first day, a great yawning chasm confronted them. What to do? Johnny Noble had faced this before, in starting his wine business. But it was one thing to buy wine, store it in the City just round the corner from potential customers for as long as necessary – the wine might even go up in value by being stored for a time – and sell it on. It was a different thing altogether to set up an oyster farm far from the market, buy in the seed oysters, work out how to grow them, and then deliver them before they went bad – always assuming you could find customers.

The two unlikely entrepreneurs recognised that it would take a while to get going. They started by making experiments with batches of larger oysters, and over some months satisfied themselves that they would grow. By chance they discovered that native oysters, which seemed the obvious choice, grew only very slowly, but the larger 'Gigas' Pacific oysters, also called rock oysters, grew rather well. Andy Lane ordered the first batch of seed oysters from Loch Creran, and built trestles on the shore to hold them in mesh bags. It fell to Johnny Noble to pay for everything.

After some months, they were worried. The oysters weren't developing – they looked more like shoehorns than oysters. Something was wrong. It turned out that the first year's supply had been poisoned by TBT, the active ingredient in antifouling paint used to prevent weed growth on ships' hulls and on salmon cages. Some of these cages were in Loch Creran, situated right beside the water inlet to the oyster hatchery. TBT is deadly to much more than seaweed. It changes the sex of dog whelks and cripples oysters. In 2003, by international agreement, it was banned on smaller craft, and in 2007 on all vessels.

They started again from the beginning. Once more they bought seed oysters with Johnny Noble's cash. And in the second year of the fledgling venture, it began to seem possible that it might work.

In the following year, 1978, since in the eyes of its two champions this was now conceivably going to be a proper business, they decided to form a company, and applied for support from the Highland and Islands Development Board (HIDB), a quango keen to promote employment in this remote area. The process of turning the original feasibility study into a full application seemed onerous in the extreme. They produced notional projections and plans about going to market, joking together about star-gazing. The people at the HIDB were delightfully endearing and chaotic; the person they were dealing with used to miss appointments regularly to have work done on his appalling teeth. Finally, however, the application was in, and the deputy chairman came to inspect the site. A vice admiral, he strode along the beach with his hands behind his back, and enthused to them about a project the HIDB was supporting to grow oysters on sticky tapes hung from rafts. He clearly viewed that as the high-tech way of the future, and the proposal to grow oysters on the shore as primitive. But to their delight the company received a grant of £30,000 and a loan of the same amount. Later it turned out that the sticky tapes, swirled by the currents, used to roll up into balls, many oysters fell off, and customers objected to struggling with great dollops of strong glue when they held the oysters to their lips.

Apart from this start-up cash, Loch Fyne Oysters Limited was born with very few assets. Johnny Noble contributed his handsome larch pleasure boat, Andy Lane his old wetsuit and a dinghy with a hole in it. That was all he had. Each took 50 per cent of the shares. The occasion provided justification for another bottle of champagne and an evening of intense discussion and slightly manic laughter in front of the fire.

To fill the gap before the first oysters matured, they decided to farm trout. Rainbow trout would do well in sea water. Andy Lane knew where they could get hold of cages. They spent much of the grant money on them, and then on the fish to go in them. Andy Lane got the cages anchored in place, helped now by David Weir, their first employee, a youngster who worked harder and drank harder than anyone in the whole of Argyll, a county peopled by hard-working and hard-drinking crofters, fishermen and estate workers.

That winter, for the first time in living memory, the sea loch froze over. The ice gripped the cages. When the tide came in, it lifted them, and when the tide went out it dragged them down the loch towards deeper water. Eventually the moving ice twisted them, tipped them over and melted, allowing the damaged cages to sink and all the fish to escape.

There was no cash left. And no product to sell. Meanwhile, David Weir's wages had to be paid. Only the £15,000 insurance money on the cages – and the occasional further contribution from Johnny Noble – saved them from bankruptcy.

Andy Lane and David Weir recovered the warped cages from the seabed, got them back in place, and restocked them with rainbow trout. That winter, the loch froze again, the fish escaped again, and the cages were completely destroyed. This time there was no insurance, and they gave up trout farming.

Instead, while waiting for the oysters to mature, they bought in prawns to sell live or cooked, herring to marinate and salmon to smoke; some were sold to local people and tourists, but they went mainly to the customers that Johnny Noble was beginning to attract in London.

The loch has never frozen since.

★

It is worth noting that Johnny Noble was risking his money *in the business.* Without it, they simply could not have functioned; they would not have been able to buy oysters, pay wages or invest in equipment. And his money was at high risk: for a year or more there was nothing but bad news, nothing at all to sell and no customers. This was heroic, entrepreneurial risk-taking at its best.

Supporters of the stock market try to make an association between on the one hand this truly creative, committed, entrepreneurial risk-taking, which builds genuinely new things; and on the other the risk that is taken when you buy shares on the stock market. They suggest that there is a similarity between the two, because the value of shares bought on the stock market can go down, and you can lose your money entirely, just as the entrepreneur can lose the money he or she puts into a new business.

But the two are not the same at all. In one case the money is in the business, helping it grow. In the other, the money never goes near the business: it is simply passed from one person to another. It is of no use whatsoever to the business. In fact, far from helping to build the business, the shares purchased carry the right to extract money from the company.

This is not investment to build businesses, it is a giant gambling game parasitic on the genuine investments and the work of others. Self-declared experts claim they can increase the chances of winning by studying the company's accounts or the patterns of graphs of stock-market trades. The argument goes that were it not for this trading of shares, no one would buy new shares – and when a company sells new shares the money does go into the company. But in fact the overall picture shows that close to 100 per cent of all business investment is funded by cash produced through operating the businesses, and by borrowings that will be repaid from cash produced in the same way. The argument that the billions of dollars used to trade shares are somehow contributing to the growth of businesses is therefore nonsense. In many years the shares on the stock market extract from the businesses quoted there more cash than they put in. Capital market theory has the stench of special pleading about it. The system has enormous vested interests − all the wealthy share owners and merchant bankers and corporate lawyers and traders and fund managers together earn huge amounts of money from it. No wonder they are drawn to the myth that investing in a business activity and 'investing' in shares are somehow similar, even equivalent.

Johnny Noble invested his money in the business, and it was very much at risk, and without it there would have been no business. That is valuable investing and no system can do without it. It benefits many more people than just the investor.

Andy Lane was painfully aware that once the grant had been used up, the cash to enable all this development had come from his partner's courage, his preparedness personally to guarantee more borrowing. The bank would not have lent a penny without Johnny Noble pledging his estate. They each owned half of the company, but his partner was taking more risk. So in an extraordinary act of generosity Andy Lane passed over a fifth of his shares, bringing Johnny Noble's holding to 60 per cent by reducing his own to 40.

This is a story of people building a business, but it is

not about greedy people trying to get away with as much as they can. It is a story of committed, creative people behaving honourably as partners. Good guys really can win.

4. Operations: The Prawn Run and the Axeman

There are some big orders for prawns today. Johnny Noble is in London, ferreting out new customers and charming existing ones with his stories. When he visits them he is as happy to engage with the chefs and the waiters as the owners, to be playing the daft laddie as often as the laird of Ardkinglas. He is well liked everywhere, and tonight there are lots of orders.

Down on the shore Andy Lane moves methodically as always, working on the oysters at low spring tide, turning and shaking the wire containers, checking for growth, looking for problems. He is fit and bursting with energy, relishing the bedlam to come as they scramble to get the prawns on the overnight train to London. There is pressure every night, but tonight is special: big orders from regular customers.

Regular business is what they have dreamed of. Andy Lane has been flinging order after order on to the overnight train at Arrochar, no time to eat, another evening gone, and at the end of it back home to the tiny but-and-ben cottage where he now lives with his dog. A mattress and a chair are his only furniture, but it is a great improvement on the decaying caravan and he is blissful there.

There is always overtime for David Graham, the driver, but still little or no money left for the two owners. Deep in himself, Andy Lane doesn't need reassurance – he knows in his gut that this will work. But for the last two years he has worked seven days a week, often twelve hours a day or more, and still the business has generated no cash – or rather, it absorbs all the cash they ever make, as they spend it on equipment and development projects. There is no time to see his Swedish girlfriend, Karen, who will go to the pub alone again this evening. He does not want to think of her there, bright-eyed men joking with her, only too ready to entertain her while he neglects her, again, to catch the tide and the train.

He hitches up his waders, finishes up on the shore about 3 p.m. and says goodbye to the oysters sinking beneath the rising tide. Then, still in his waders, he calls in at the decrepit old building where the handful of employees – more like friends, really – prepare the herring and salmon.

It is time to get the prawns. Working back, they will have to leave by 7 p.m. for the 8.15 sleeper train. If they are lucky and drive like maniacs they will have an hour at base to unload up to a quarter of a tonne of prawns, weigh out the orders, cook a proportion of them, package them up, and mark up the boxes with all the information needed to get them to their destinations. If the order is for cooked prawns, they will plunge the poor creatures into Steaming Edna to boil for exactly three minutes. The boiler lies in the open, not far from the pickling shed, under the trees, sheltered from the prying eyes of officialdom. No rates are paid and no health officials are aware of the various fish-pickling and smoking activities going on in these secluded buildings, overgrown with ivy and surrounded by banks of nettles. The whole place looks as if it should be infested with rats and mice, but the wild mink kill everything that moves – they also steal the occasional fish, but that is judged a fair price for keeping the area rodent-free.

Chris Brown, the prawn fisherman, is expected to dock at Crinan, a picturesque small port some 40 miles away, often an hour's drive, with the last 5 miles among the most dangerous of any road in Britain: single-track, twisting through the trees along the canal, and the locals driving like maniacs, not used to meeting anyone on the road, apparently content to treat emergency stops as a normal part of travelling.

Andy Lane goes into the office and phones Portpatrick Radio, who put him through to the boat on a VHF link. He always buys the whole catch, which can vary hugely in weight. Any extra is cooked and frozen. He tries to gauge from their exchange whether the catch is a good one, but every boat up and down the coast can hear their conversation, so as usual nothing is disclosed. Of the only two phrases ever used by the fisherman, 'Not too bad' is reassuring – the other is 'Not too good', but that can be used simply to cover his tracks, the two phrases being almost interchangeable. He is due to arrive at Crinan at about 5 p.m. – they have to leave now.

Outside, Andy Lane calls David Graham, and they drive off in the pickup.

The health authorities, if they knew about it, would worry about this van. It carries everything – raw fish and cooked shellfish, encrusted implements from the oyster farm and clean instruments for the herring marinades and the smokery. Tonight it will carry fish boxes filled with live prawns and later some filled with live prawns and others with cooked, the boxes randomly stacked on top of one another. There will be no time to wash out the van at any stage, and it does not occur to anyone that this should be done. There is barely time to catch the train, and anyway it all seems so clean – prawns fresh from the sea, cooked briefly in a great boiler that looks a bit rusty on the outside, to be sure, but gleams inside. Besides, sea water is a great antiseptic.

There are other authorities, too, who might worry about the van – if they knew of David Graham's drinking habits. When Andy Lane moved to the west of Scotland he was amazed to discover that to fit in as a normal person you have to down quantities of alcohol that would impress the most hardened of drinkers down south. He was goggle-eyed the first time he spent an evening in the pub with David Graham. Not long afterwards he had to pull him out of the ditch, and on another occasion early one winter morning he found him unconscious, his overcoat frozen to the road. But Andy Lane has been reassured over time, watching with incredulous fascination as David Graham never starts drinking before 6.30 and always stops at 10.30 sharp, no matter what the temptations and pressures he faces. The problem is the quantity he manages to imbibe between those fixed hours. But his work rarely suffers and in the morning he always seems able to drive.

His conversation is filled with stories from a colourful past.

Doing photography with a monkey on Blackpool promenade, I had a franchise from six of the big hotels and made loads of money. I mean, £200 a day in the 1950s – that was good money if like me you were just out of the armed forces. I bought three flats there. The monkey

became alcoholic, drinking when I was out taking group
pictures. In the morning he had the severe DTs. I used
to have to give him a wee drop just to steady him up.
He was smoking too.

The drinking, smoking monkey was not the end of it.
There were tales from the time he owned an antique
business, and others about the rabbit farm. Then there
was the gamekeeping.

I've been with four Lords and a Duke at the gamekeeping.
I was stalking up in Knoydart and Jura before that. So in
the larder I was very good with a knife. Many, many
years ago I was on the Ross estate, Ross who invented
the Ross rifle – it's Al Fayed's 'Balnagowan' now. One
of my guests was James Stewart, the film star. That was a
memorable one, half a dozen days with Jimmy Stewart.
He'd been shooting bears in Russia before he came to
me. He was quick on the trigger. As a young stalker you
couldn't start better than that, could you?

And he was successful, it seemed, at the art of seduction
too. Harry Corbett, the presenter of *Sooty*, a TV puppet
show for children, had installed his Spanish mistress in
Blackpool.

I started a wee affair with her. That wasn't very proper
at the time.

He ended up in a wee *fracas* over that.
The pressure is on, and Andy Lane drives fast. The
road is familiar, the same road that he takes to go to the

pub in Ardfern. Loch Fyne speeds by on the left as the sun sets ahead in yet another spectacular red sky over the islands. In winter the light has faded by the time they reach the dangerous single-track road among the trees; the headlights make it safer, warning each speeding vehicle of the other long before they come head to head round blind corners. But this is summer, and they have two near misses along the canal-side.

They arrive at Crinan in time to see the boat dock gently. With the nimbleness of honed expertise her crew swing the boxes of prawns in sets of four on to the side. Andy Lane eyes the hold from the edge of the pier. It seems unusually full, and with big prawns too.

'Is that what you call "not bad" now, Chris? Looks bloody marvellous.'

'Aye, Andy, not bad, not bad. There's over forty stone there, and the sizes are pretty well OK.'

It is a record quantity, not bad indeed. In twenty minutes of back-breaking work the van is loaded. Then the cash is settled and they are off again, leaving a wet trail behind them.

Once, picking up the prawns by himself, David Graham forgets to fix the back flap of the pickup van. Arriving back at base, he finds that the van is empty. The boxes of prawns have fallen out at intervals along the road home. A crazed dash in the van recovers most, if not all, of them.

Tonight, back at Cairndow, they announce their arrival on the van's strident horn, and once again it is all hands on deck, carrying boxes of prawns to empty into the boiling cauldron or to package up for the live orders. Soon the cooked prawns are cooling in water and the boxes stand ready labelled, each one to take a different weight to a different destination. By the time they arrive in London they will have been transformed by Johnny Noble's panache into the 'finest native langoustines, the freshest in the land'. Which they are, really.

Andy Lane chivvies everyone along, the refilled boxes are packaged and loaded, and once again he and David Graham set off, this time turning away from the loch towards Arrochar. The van careers over the Rest and Be Thankful Pass, down the long straight between towering mountains still clearly visible in the twilight of the northern summer evening, and eventually swerves up the short track below the tiny station. The train has not yet arrived, which is just as well since with all these boxes they will need time to get ready. They unload and stack some on to the British Rail handcart they recently persuaded the stationmaster to let them use. Then they push it up the steep path, across the rails and along the platform to where the guard's van will stop, so that they can stow them swiftly when the train comes. Then quickly down again for the next set. The train has more than once left before giving them time to load all the boxes. As a precaution, once the van is empty they collect the second handcart and park it across the railway line. The train won't be leaving without the boxes tonight.

Soon the puffing steam train pulls in and the guard steps out. The guard's van is padlocked.

'Can we have the keys, please? We've got these boxes to load.'

'I can't find the keys.'

The tone suggests bloody-mindedness rather than apology. It is the voice of the state servant, pleased to work

in a nationalised industry, concerned mainly to insist on
following rules, particularly where it is annoying to others,
and with no interest in serving these ordinary people in
front of him.

Andy Lane and David Graham look at each other. It
would take for ever to load each box separately through
a passenger door and manhandle it along the tight corri-
dor. The train will not wait. But these are not prawns
set out in a national plan, with no one caring if they
reach their destination or rot on the platform. These
prawns are the heart of their business. Their very existence, so it feels, depends on getting these prawns delivered
to London.

Andy Lane pulls himself up to his full, imposing height.
'David!' he says in a sergeant-major voice. 'Where's the
axe?'

And turning to the guard, 'That'll get the lock off, no
bother. We'll get you into your van.' His tone is helpful,
in a man-to-man kind of way. Anyone could get into a
pickle like this, it seems to say, but we will help you
get out of it. We'll smash the lock and if necessary the
door too.

David Graham understands and goes purposefully to
the van. There is no axe and he knows it, but he rummages
noisily in the back of the vehicle. The guard lifts his cap
and scratches his head.

'Hang on a minute, I'll just have another look for that
key,' he says.

And soon the keys have materialised.

They step into the guard's van eagerly, and shift parcels
and bicycles to make space for their precious prawns. For
the third time in a few hours, sweating and grunting, they

swing the boxes across. After they are loaded Andy Lane gives the paperwork to the guard.

'You'll see these are for London,' he says, looking straight into his face. 'Not the Midlands.' They both know that twice the guards have left on the platform at Crewe fish destined for London, and that claims have been registered successfully with British Rail. But payments from British Rail don't matter to the guard, nor to the customers who waited in vain for their prawns and held Loch Fyne Oysters responsible.

The engine driver gives a long blast on the whistle.

They trot along to drag the handcart off the rails, then as the train pulls out they wander down to the van.

'Got him this time!'

'Did you see his face when you called for the axe?'

Back at base in the now dark and empty building, Andy Lane pickles some herring, takes the orders from the telex and writes down more that have been left on the answering machine. Then at last it is time for a roll-up and a glass of the cheap, raw Don Pablo pickling sherry. Nearly every night, to the wonderment of the locals, the lights stay on until after ten. Then, after a quick visit to the pub, to listen to the crack from the characters of Cairndow, Andy Lane goes back with his dog to his tiny cottage and falls into an exhausted sleep.

No one said it would be easy.

5. Brand Marketing: a Party and Walruses

By 1984 the supplies of oysters, herring, salmon, langoustines and scallops were reliable, as dependable as harvesting seafood ever is, and Andy Lane had honed the operations into a viable system, albeit one that never felt quite under control. The evolving dream of providing local seafood, caught using sustainable methods, was beginning to work well. They could control the purity of the shellfish they farmed themselves, of course, and they were buying the langoustines from Chris Brown because he caught them in pots. The difference in quality between pot-caught and trawler-caught prawns was palpable, and the effect on the seabed was radically better. The same went for the scallops – those picked off the seabed individually by divers were being harvested on a sustainable basis, whereas the scallop trawlers left devastation in their wake. The salmon too was sourced from the most ecologically advanced farms. The commitment to sustainability was taking practical shape.

Johnny Noble decided that the business was ready for its next stage: all of humankind should be made aware of it. He resolved with his usual disregard for risk to spend some more money, this time in a way that would allow him to play to his strengths. Recognising that launching Loch Fyne Oysters on the world required above all to attract a bit of attention, he did what came naturally – he organised a party. Ardkinglas House had seen many parties, and Johnny Noble was at his best acting the bountiful host, master of the grand house beside the loch among the mountains, dispensing good humour, good whisky and even better wines in liberal measures. His shyness would disappear, his voice booming down the great stone staircase to welcome each arrival with genuine delight and warmth.

However, he knew that he would struggle to convince key people to come to the party, and struggle even more to fund it. Undaunted, he convinced Bollinger champagne's UK agents, and the owners of *Decanter* magazine, that their interests would be well served by adding their names to the event, and by funding the trip in cash and in kind.

To this party he invited a selection of the most famous chefs and food writers in Britain. The guests included David Shepherd, who together with the actor Michael Caine owned Langan's, one of London's top restaurants; Fay Maschler, restaurant critic and a towering figure in the food trade; Jane Grigson, food critic for the *Observer* and author of the Penguin book on *Fish Cookery*; and Derek Cooper, who had started the *Food Programme* on BBC radio. They were grandees in their own right and did not need to reply to the many invitations that arrived on a daily basis, but the lure of oysters and champagne at Loch Fyne hooked them.

At the loch there would be nothing much to show them. There was the embryonic salmon smokery hidden in a half-ruined building. In the open among the trees there was Steaming Edna, the rusty-looking old boiler used for cooking prawns and langoustines. The office was just a room in an outhouse. Even the oysters looked pretty decrepit, nothing to see but black mesh bags lying on frames, visible only when the tide went out. And when the tide was out the loch was at its least pleasing, with smells of rotting seaweed drifting over the wide shore.

Johnny Noble was not in the least deterred.

Most of the guests were arriving late in the evening. Booming and smiling, he poured as a nightcap after the champagne the largest drams of single malt whisky that they had ever seen. They would need a bit of shut-eye after their journey, he explained.

Low tide the following day was early in the morning. He arranged for brunch to start comfortably late. It proved a leisurely meal with, among other delicacies, porridge, kippers, scrambled eggs, smoked salmon, langoustines, velvet crabs, champagne and, of course, oysters. The oysters were pure, as Johnny Noble emphasised, but they were not purified: in later years the company would invest significant amounts of money in state-of-the-art 'depuration' systems for extracting any dangerous bacteria from the oysters, but these were hardier days and they came fresh from the beach. Meanwhile the tide was covering the beach, and also the oysters. Well after midday, interrupting the free-flowing bonhomie that he generated so effortlessly, Johhny Noble took his guests to the great bay window overlooking the loch. Pointing towards the huge trees all round and to the loch below, he invited them to join him on an expedition to the shore. More time was spent equipping everyone with boots and jackets, and then at last they stood at the lochside.

It was high tide. Of the growing oysters there was nothing to be seen.

With a magnificent gesture, Johnny Noble launched

into a tour de force of imaginative word painting, conjuring before them first storms, then oysters. They were lucky to have come on a day like this; calm airs and warm sunshine were not typical in these hills. Literally millions of oysters lay beneath the surface, all of them belonging to Loch Fyne Oysters. And all of them feasting contentedly on the rich, pure Loch Fyne plankton that abounded there, absorbing natural nutrients and putting on the pounds, or the ounces rather, as if they could sense that their lives would be short. Short, but particularly beneficial, even magical, for older gentlemen.

He looked at his guests. They were listening, rapt. Champagne and stories for breakfast, now a speech in the sunshine by the loch. Wonderful.

Andy Lane, standing at the edge of the group, marvelled at the performance. He felt and looked a little ungainly, out of his waders and away from his natural habitat. He was happier working alone with the oysters at low tide than being charming to distinguished strangers at high tide. But Johnny Noble in full swing was a spectacle to behold.

He moved on to talk about oyster lore, which he persuaded his guests was based soundly in the experience of generations. The oyster was one of the most concentrated sources of minerals available in the human quest for the perfect food. They had a bit of everything – zinc, copper, calcium, iodine – you name it, the Loch Fyne oyster had it. And minerals were what people, particularly men, needed. No wonder Aphrodite had chosen an oyster shell in which to give birth to Eros. They had worked their magic for Casanova too, to the satisfaction of many a good lady.

Johnny Noble's eyes twinkled, but he did not linger on that subject. He was shy about sex. His sister Christina speculated that his lifelong lack of involvement with any partner might have been due to being terribly hurt in an early relationship. He was constantly filling the great house with all kinds of people of all ages and both sexes, and many described him as a deeply attractive man, full of good humour, always ready for an impish laugh, sincerely interested in what each person had to say, able to talk about anything under the sun, full of unlikely stories that sometimes had people howling with laughter. But there was never any evidence of an intimate relationship.

And when others regaled him with stories laced with innuendo, he became visibly embarrassed. In later years he dealt regularly in London with a wholesaler who had an appetite for life that matched his own. Although he was married, and his wife well known to Johnny Noble and liked by him, this man seemed to have a stream of lovers, and to judge by the winking and gestures that he made, their key features always included large breasts. He was more than willing to go into far too much detail about his encounters with them. He also told very bad risqué jokes. Johnny Noble clearly found these exchanges excruciating, not just because he felt loyal to the man's wife, but because he was expected to laugh knowingly. This was the one subject on which he did not respond story for story.

If Johnny Noble had no love life that anyone could see, he did not seem to lose by it. People accepted it without question, partly because he was never miserable. As far as anyone could see, he was fine without a lover. He was so much his own person that you could not imagine setting him up with a potential partner. It just wouldn't have worked, and no one tried.

At the lochside, however, this entertaining, intriguing, lovable man seemed anything but shy. With gesticulations and facial expressions worthy of the most uninhibited actor, he was painting a picture more beautiful by far than the reality, of oysters energetically absorbing and purifying the ingredients that make men potent.

It was not just the famous minerals that we get from these fantastic molluscs, nurtured on the rich and pure sediments of Loch Fyne, he said. They also gave us vitamins. Again, names rolled off his tongue, pregnant with an almost ceremonial significance: riboflavin; niacin; thiamin; ascorbic acid; calciferol. The list went on. These were the vitamins that put a sparkle in your eye. All these were found, along with the minerals and other good things, in Loch Fyne oysters.

He continued to divert his audience with oyster lore. Oysters were a staple of the diet of the artisans and tradesmen who built the great factories in the pandemonium of the early industrial revolution. The filthy streets of Edinburgh echoed to the cries of the Oyster Lassies, selling them for a farthing a poke. The prices were controlled by the city authorities, and the oystermen would guard the beds jealously. In 1788 the oyster fleets of Newhaven and Prestonpans came to blows, fighting a sea battle near the Black Rocks in the Forth. After serious wounds inflicted on both sides, but thankfully no fatalities, the victorious Newhaven oystermen towed their opponents' boats back home in triumph. The captured oysters were sold round the streets of Edinburgh for one shilling a 100, very similar to their price a century earlier. In real terms, allowing for inflation, Johnny Noble said, that was very similar to the present-day price.

He also sketched for them the philosophy on which the building of the business was based. The guiding principle was one of respect for the 'animal' and its habitat. They sought to ensure that the environmental impact of their activities was at worst neutral. They were working actively to enhance biodiversity in the seas, by insisting that their suppliers fished only with nature-friendly methods. They wanted to underpin the economy of the local community by providing skilled work, fairly rewarded and in line with the traditions of the locality. And in a world dominated by global brands and multinationals, they were committed to maintaining a market for independent producers like Chris Brown, who had provided the excellent langoustines served at breakfast, using sustainable methods to get the best possible quality on to the table. For example, they did not buy any supplies landed by trawlers, which devastated the seabed and mashed the fish. This meant that sometimes the company had to buy white fish from Iceland, which had more progressive and effective policies than the UK. But the local supplies of seafood from line-fishing and pots were the best in Europe. It was time to recognise Scottish seafood for what it was – the best.

To his audience, this was unfamiliar thinking. But expressed with conviction and passion, with a confident twinkle in the eye and backed up by detailed answers to the questions that they asked, it was utterly convincing. This was good stuff indeed.

Packed off in the afternoon on their long journeys home, carrying bags of delicacies and bottles of good

wine, the guests never saw anything to do with the production of oysters or other seafood, or indeed anything
else other than the view. But they were filled with warm
memories of the stories and the whisky, champagne and
wine in Ardkinglas House.

Over the next few weeks the name of Loch Fyne
Oysters began to appear in the press, and some of the
best restaurants placed their first orders. From the outset
the name had overtones that any brand manager would
die for. Quality. Freshness. Natural zest. Purity. Wildness.
Aphrodisiac power. Highland beauty.

Jane Grigson wrote in the *Observer*:

> I was extra delighted to come across a Scottish hero of
> what one hopes is an incipient fish revolution, John
> Noble of Ardkinglas in Argyll. At Ardkinglas the blend
> of salt and fresh water from the rivers Kinglas and Fyne
> is just right for oysters. Purity is absolute.

Johnny Noble's courage and wit had got things moving,
and he never let up. Year after year a stream of customers
got the Ardkinglas treatment and the speech on the shore
at high tide. He once turned down an invitation to eat
with American friends because he was committed to
cooking dinner for twelve French chefs. It was not in his
nature to become fixed in any role, such as that of the
Grand Host as opposed to a cook in the kitchen, nor to
play safe – testing his culinary skills on French chefs was
not a coward's way. He was indefatigable in searching
for ways to promote Loch Fyne Oysters, and had many
successes over the next fifteen years.

In 1999 another opportunity arose. Johnny Noble was

not alone in his sense of mischief. The proprietor of the neighbouring estate along the loch, Sir Charles Maclean, owned the Creggans Inn at Strachur. Conversations during his visits to Ardkinglas were wide-ranging – Johnny Noble read voraciously and Charles Maclean had founded the *Ecologist* magazine in the 1970s. In 1999 he formed a dining club, named 'for no good reason' the Walrus Club. Johnny Noble would provide the oysters for their dinners.

Soon after one of the club's highly convivial meetings, a gossip column in a London newspaper suggested that this was a cover for a group of people who wished to turn loose a number of walruses in Loch Fyne. The story caught the popular imagination. Charles Maclean was reported as saying that since the last walrus on the west coast of Scotland had been killed as recently as 1846 they would certainly thrive and be a great boon for the tourist trade. They would also provide educational stimulation for the local children.

Johnny Noble was flamboyantly outraged. The wide stone corridors of Ardkinglas House echoed with denunciations of the walrus. After a period of honing, his complaints began to land on the desks of the editors of national and local newspapers. The *Sunday Times* proclaimed, 'Loch Plunged into Walrus War'; the *Dunoon Observer* headlined with delight, 'Lairds on Walrus Collision Course'. Johnny Noble was quoted as saying that he wanted to remain on good terms with his neighbouring estate owner, but these creatures ate a colossal amount of bivalves. They would live on them, hoovering up the innocent shellfish into their ravening maws. Loch Fyne's oyster-beds, the home of the purest oysters in Britain, could be destroyed. As evidence he quoted Lewis Carroll's poem 'The Walrus and the Carpenter'.

The rumour was received with horror by the fishermen, by Scottish Natural Heritage and by the Loch Fyne Marine Trust. Introduction of a non-native species would contravene the Wildlife and Countryside Act and would be subject to heavy fines. What would happen if a clam diver came up against one of these 2-tonne monsters, which could eat 6000 clams, oysters and mussels in one go? Humourless pontification from authorities stimulated Johnny Noble's glee at the absurdity. There wasn't much going on at the time, and the story was picked up by national news programmes on TV and radio. Visitor numbers rose, to seek out the oysters and, prematurely, the walruses. Neither proved easy to find.

On the occasion of Charles Maclean's next visit to Ardkinglas the corridors were filled until long after midnight with muffled reverberations from the library, where Johnny Noble often drank whisky by the fire with his favourite guests. They were the sounds of joyful voices and bursts of sustained, apparently uncontrollable laughter.

No one knows if Charles Maclean ever actually took steps towards obtaining a walrus. However, the virtual walruses brought such publicity for the oysters in Loch Fyne that this more than compensated, in Johnny Noble's mind, for the depredations their ancestor-walrus had committed in Lewis Caroll's poem.

Consumer marketing surveys in 2006 showed that a remarkably high proportion of people in the UK recognised the name Loch Fyne Oysters. Recognition had started with the food writers' visit to the loch at high tide, and continued growing right through to the walrus threat and beyond, into the new millennium.

When he wasn't entertaining guests at Ardkinglas, Johnny Noble was out in the wider world drumming up business, and typically having glorious fun doing it. There were regular, and successful, trips to Hong Kong and the United States, as well as to Europe. Wherever he went, he made friends, and orders usually followed.

It was hard work as well as fun. Later, he recruited the twenty-four-year-old Rosie Bleazard to help him, organizing his sales trips, accompanying him on many of them and following up as required afterwards – not his forte. In fact, as things turned out, much of Rosie Bleazard's time had to be spent on non-sales activity.

Johnny used to come in in a fluster, regularly, with the name and address of somebody who had found his brief-case. He used to put his briefcase on the roof of his car and then drive off. Somebody would find it and get in touch. At one stage it seemed to be all I ever did.

His distracted approach extended also to driving. Luckily Rosie Bleazard was not in the car when he drove over the edge of the twisty road along the side of Loch Lomond. Though the bank was steep and the car ended up with its bonnet under water, Johnny Noble was fine.

She remembers an early trip abroad with him, to an exhibition in Brussels.

We arrived at Glasgow airport, the two of us, and nearly all the British Airways staff knew him. 'Morning, Mr Noble!' 'How are you today, Mr Noble?' And he was

waving his passport, 'I've got it, I've got it!' He had on
previous occasions turned up without it, so it seemed to
be a bit of a joke. He was just so well known. We got on
the flight and took off, and then heard on the intercom,
'Could everyone please check their pockets?' A lady on
her way to Dublin was missing her car keys. Johnny just
looked at me and said, 'It's me. I don't even have to look.
It's me, I've done it.' And he pulled out her keys. He'd
just blindly picked up whatever was in the plate at
security.

But his absent-mindedness did not extend to conversation.

He was such a gentleman and such a lovely, lovely person.
He knew something about everything. He could start up
a conversation with anyone in a room, and no matter
what they came out with he could have an informed
conversation with them about it, rather than just grunting. He knew someone or he'd read something – he
could take the conversation forward on any subject. It was
fascinating. But general memory issues he really struggled
with. His brain was just operating elsewhere, doing things
that were more important to him.

His consumption of 'pop' was the same on sales trips
as at home.

He always had a glass of wine. 'A meal without wine is
like a day without sunshine,' he used to say, a quote he'd
picked up somewhere. It fitted his life.

His personality did not change with drink, even though sometimes he reached the point of not being able to find reverse in his own car – an automatic.

If we'd had a few too many he never ever showed a side to me that was aggressive. He was always a very happy, very gentlemanly, very polite man. If anything there was an extra twinkle in his eye, and that was just a sense of fun, just a bit more cheeky. He was always a great, great, lovely, lovely man. And such a laugh to travel with.

Rick Stein, one of the best-known seafood chefs in the UK and further afield, fronted a television series that included a meal cooked with Johnny Noble in the kitchen at Ardkinglas. As is true of so many people, famous or ordinary, his memories of Johnny Noble, related to me in 2007, are vivid and warm.

Johnny was probably the most passionate and knowledge-able devotee of seafood I've ever met. He lived for his oysters – to him they weren't just a bite of the sea but a taste of home. Often after filming we'd chat for hours about seafood and the state of fishing in Loch Fyne. He was very concerned at the time by the big trawlers coming into the loch to trawl for langoustines. He really felt for the local creel fishermen in their small boats with their baited pots. They didn't stand a chance against the trawlers – to him it was like driving a massive bulldozer through a prized garden. Thanks to him, I suspect, that doesn't happen any longer. I just hope there are passionate people like him working in the Government today helping to protect our fishing interests.

His love for seafood knew no bounds, and he was also a great trencherman. One of his sayings was, 'A roast goose is too much for one and not enough for two,' and one of his favourite dishes was boiled mutton with caper sauce. I'd never tried it before I met him but I've had it loads of times since and every time I can see his beaming face filling up my glass with claret.

6. Blazing a Trail

Andy Lane had not expected it to be easy, and sometimes it really wasn't.

Building a business is not a difficult thing in principle. Once you have a good idea the rest is common sense. It is self-evident that you have to give customers what they want – no one will part with money for something that is not attractive. So you have to find out what pleases them. If possible, you can even shape what they want – Johnny Noble seemed to have the instinct for that. If you sell them something that displeases them, it is obvious that you have to take care of them; if you don't, they won't come back, and they will spread their dissatisfaction, undermining your reputation. When you sell something, you clearly have to charge enough to cover your costs; that means raising prices whenever you can, and always keeping your costs down. Simple stuff.

But as soon as you start putting these uncomplicated principles into practice, you find that *nothing* is simple. It is a battle to achieve a fair price even for the best smoked salmon in the world. And what does it cost, anyway? That depends on how much is produced – if the smokery can be kept going all the time, each side of salmon works out cheaper. But all the costs of idle time must be built in, and also something extra charged, towards the day when the old smokery will be replaced with new state-of-the-art

equipment. And so on. Distinguished careers in accounting are built on these questions.

Meanwhile, the entrepreneur has to solve every single
problem that arises: someone can't make it today to serve
in the shop; the tractor has broken down; a new contact
is promising a big order but we would have to reduce
the price; what are we going to call that new product? A
big customer has asked for more time to pay his latest
invoice: if we agree, will we manage to pay the wages
next week? And if we don't agree, will he just not pay
on time anyway?

Judgement, decision; judgement, decision – with rarely
enough information, and no time to think.

For Andy Lane, the pressure sometimes became in-
tolerable. When Johnny Noble was there it was better,
because they could talk anything through. But Johnny
Noble was sometimes away for weeks on end, leaving
Andy Lane to run the place by himself. Frustration would
build up.

> Quite often I would rail and mentally gnash my teeth
> and bite the carpet when there was nobody else there.

There were no serious consequences of ranting in
private. But privacy was not guaranteed. The Highlands
of Scotland have always attracted a great variety of visitors.
In the early days of the oyster farm, David Sheppard, the
Bishop of Liverpool, came to stay nearby. Well known at
the time as one of the Church leaders opposed to the
policies of Margaret Thatcher's Government, he was co-
author of the 1985 Church of England report *Faith in the*

City, which blamed increasing inner-city deprivation on Thatcherite policies. The report became celebrated when it was dismissed by one cabinet minister as 'pure Marxist theology'. The Bishop himself was a gentle person, and one summer he stayed with his wife for an extended time in a cottage near Loch Fyne.

One day Andy Lane took the tractor down to the beach, with the buck-rake used to lift the oyster frames.

> I'd gone down to catch the tide, and something had bust, so the buck-rake had come off the back of the tractor. I was trying to get it back on and I was getting more and more mad, because the tide was coming in, time was running out. And I remember just kicking it. Absolute Basil Fawlty, when he beat up his car with a bush – it was just like that. I was kicking it, 'You fucking buck-rake!' Kick! Kick! And up there at the top of the shore, just watching, were this saintly couple, hand in hand, looking at this everyday, typical moment of a peaceful pastoral life.

Sometimes other people inside the company bore the brunt of his desperation.

> I used to stomp and swear, and people used to think I was mad with them. I was not mad with them, I was mad with myself.

What surfaced unpredictably in the mind of Andy Lane also included decisions of intuitive and principled genius. Without them Loch Fyne Oysters would not have been so far ahead of its time. But to be ahead of one's time entails acting in ways that are not respected, and are even ridiculed, at the time.

There was the commitment to sell seafood only if it had been caught using sustainable methods. Andy Lane:

> We were seen as nutters for years. This was never going to work; it was a joke. We weren't taken seriously. Which was fine, because in some ways it's nice to be unconventional.

If his heart told him that what he was doing was right, he was always prepared to be seen as a nutter. Christine MacCallum, running the shop at Loch Fyne Oysters, recalls one episode that illustrates this. Andy Lane came into the shop in his waders, as usual. He had recently given up smoking. Without any pause for small talk he pointed at the cigarette machine in the corner. 'Take it out!' he said.

Christine MacCallum was astounded. The company's profits seemed precarious, and one of the most dependable sources of cash was the cigarette machine. Andy Lane's particular beef was that its biggest customers were the staff, and it was killing them. But outside customers came in for tobacco too, and when they did, they had a look at the other things in the shop; some ended up spending quite a bit on marinated herring or kippers or salmon or oysters. So it wasn't just the cash from tobacco they would lose: tobacco sales led to seafood sales. And some of the people who came in to buy seafood took the opportunity to stock up on cigarettes while they were there. The profitability of the shop would be affected.

She protested. He insisted.

When the supplier came to top up the cigarettes in the machine, he was poleaxed. He knew how much the cigarette machine was earning, and had never seen anyone throw one out. Christine MacCallum still feels the horror of that moment as she talks of it, but she sees it differently now:

Everywhere now is catching up, twenty years on.

Sustainable fishing, good for people, good for nature; healthy living, not encouraging addiction to smoking; on these Andy Lane took a stand.

Another important moment was when he reacted against what he regarded as the abuse of power. Again, in doing so, he went against all the normal rules for making a business successful.

Loch Fyne Oysters had won a contract to supply oysters to Tesco, increasingly the dominant supermarket chain in the UK. It had been hard to win, and with Johnny Noble's enthusiastic lead they had celebrated the victory with champagne. The contract provided good steady business, if at low margins.

But the relationship was not one of equals, nor even of senior and junior partners.

We'd go down to Tesco head office in wherever it was. There was a horrible atmosphere of fear. You'd see all the suppliers lining up, their jobs and lives depending on it. I thought the whole relationship was ghastly, I fell prey to recurring nightmares about negotiating with the SS.

Then they became more and more and more demanding, and they started to do more and more promotions with oysters, and we always paid. And the final straw came one day when we'd been down to London to see them and the next day we got a phone call to say 'By the way we're doing another promotion at 25 per cent off.'

We always said we didn't want to do these things. So we said we weren't going to do it. They insisted and it went backwards and forwards. And I had this uncomfortable feeling that if we gave in to these people we'd have sold our souls. Then the high heidyin of the department came on the phone, to say that we had to do it, and I ended up saying, 'No, we won't. And actually, you can fuck off!'

We pulled out, and I'm very glad we did. By saying no we won back our souls. I felt that if we'd caved in we'd have lost them for ever.

At a personal level the stress told on Andy Lane. Not only was he the man who had to resolve everything, make all the difficult decisions himself and work seven days a week; he also took the strain of setting a wholly independent course, ignoring and going against the normal dictates of business, in order to create a new kind of principled business.

He dealt with the pressure as best he could. Walking alone in the hills with his dog helped.

Up the glen there is a quality of silence that is just fabulous. I spent a short time in the Little Karoo in South Africa, and it's the same. That kind of dense silence, which is actually full of life. There are animals out there, and stars: there's just a big impact of real wild nature. It was mind-blowing, being a part of that, able to wander the hills and never see a soul. I just love being at the tops of hills, in complete isolation.

But seven years after the start he found himself getting depressed.

At one point, about 1984, I started to get really run down. I didn't know what it was, but I got seriously depressed. I ended up in clinical depression. I always had a slight melancholic tendency, but that got really tough. I didn't take drugs for it. I didn't take drugs for almost anything – I didn't believe in it. And I didn't fancy going to a psychiatrist or anything like that. But it made life extremely hard, because you had to hide it.

There were compensations.

The other side of the coin was all this frenetic energy. It was almost manic. I used to bounce from one thing to the other. But it didn't stop me getting stuck, in really bad depression.

The business at least gave him a relentless, unavoidable reason to get up in the morning.

Very often it would take me about two hours to get out in the morning, so I had to get up really early just to get myself going.

★

Whether it was part of the problem or part of what kept him sane, there was something else going on in his head as he ran the business. At the times when he was really angry an imaginary fellow-MD used to appear, like a genie out of a bottle. The role of the genie was to take the blame.

I was largely mad with myself, but I wasn't entirely mad with myself. For years I thought the company was run by somebody else. I didn't quite know who it was, but basically it was an idiot.

He laughs, quite gently, the corners of his eyes crinkling. There is no evidence of mania.

It was a psychological trick, which must have taken the pressure off. I used to think, 'Well, it's not my bloody fault!' and 'This place is run by a nutcase!' When things went wrong it would so piss me off, I would think, 'Why the fuck are you working for this company?' as if this imaginary friend of mine had got it all wrong.

He chuckles again.

I would rail against the circumstances and rail against the powers that be whoever they were, because they were absolutely stupid. But it got me through.

Eventually he contacted a counsellor.

It had a happy ending in a way, because I looked in the Yellow Pages for a counsellor in Glasgow. I went to see her, and she was just not at all what I expected: not at all conventional, pretty exotic, dyed blonde hair, in her early fifties, red pullover, tartan skirt, full of life.

The second time I went to see her she gave me a drink. Then she came up and stayed with me one weekend, and we drank quite a lot. So this wasn't conventional counselling. She probably should have been dispassionate but she wasn't a bit. I just talked to her. She was great; she made me laugh. She used to tell me her problems as well, and we became real mates, actually. And that helped get me out of this despond.

I wrestled with depression for some years. But the hard part was hiding it from people.

There was no refuge to be had in religion, though as he emerged from depression he discovered the benefits of meditation.

I had always wanted to be attracted by the Church but was largely repelled by it as an institution. I always craved authenticity. I read a book about Tibetan Buddhism, and went to a week-long Buddhist retreat in Somerset. I was struck by the authenticity of the Tibetan Lama, the robustness, the strength, the guts of it all, and yet the complete lack of ego. It started me learning meditation, which was an extension of this sort of oneness in wild places. You get this greater sense of stillness within yourself. And then all this crud that happens in your head is just crud. You realise you're doing it. I think I'd been beset by crud for years, and that was one thing that I was railing against and angry about.

★

The relationship between Andy Lane and Johnny Noble was vital to them both, and to the business. With two such strong and different characters working so intensely together, it is not surprising that the relationship was occasionally strained. On a few occasions, Andy Lane actually resigned.

> Johnny and I would get absolutely at loggerheads about something. Often it was quite probably not very significant at all. I would just take umbrage. I don't know how many times I resigned – two or three, I think.

In 1990 they decided that it would probably help them and the business if they brought a non-executive director on to the board – someone who would bring professional standards, experienced business judgement, a wise head, and perhaps some financial skills as well. Johnny asked around to identify likely candidates. Two trusted friends in banking independently recommended Bob Craig, an ex-naval commander and qualified accountant, somewhat older than both the founders, with a good and varied track record of involvement in business. He had worked extensively with small companies facing insolvency, helping them avoid bankruptcy if possible, with the result that he knew well the problems small businesses could face. One of the attractions was that he lived in Campbeltown, on the Mull of Kintyre, which meant that most weeks he drove past the door of Loch Fyne Oysters anyway. He would be able to keep in touch easily, not just disappear between board meetings.

A little later Gordon Davidson, a canny Glasgow businessman, was spotted by Andy Lane working as a consultant for a Scottish shellfish-marketing group. The group's meetings always seemed about to degenerate into fully-fledged punch-ups, and Andy Lane admired the robust but kindly way Gordon Davidson brought some order to them. When he joined Loch Fyne Oysters, initially as a consultant and later as a non-executive director, he made a difference immediately, establishing some basic monthly accounts so that they could tell if they were making or losing money, and roughly to what extent. Bob Craig then used these to create quarterly financial accounts. This was a novelty: so far Johnny Noble and Andy Lane had only found out how much they had made or (often) lost when they got the accounts from the auditor eleven months after the end of the year. Bob Craig:

> They knew how they were doing only through their ability to pay their bills and meet the wages. They had really been through the tough bit before I came – they'd got the thing stabilised. But they certainly knew the problems of running out of cash, so one of the first tasks was to start getting management accounts installed, and some system of reporting and recording.

As well as instilling more professional corporate behaviour – regular minuted meetings, procedures to meet the requirements of company and employment law, proper handling of conflicts of interest – Bob Craig sometimes acted as a go-between for the two main characters, helping to resolve or smooth over the difficult issues.

> They didn't like to clash, but they were completely different personalities. More than once Andy actually

resigned. Once I said to Johnny, 'I'm glad we've got through that phase now.' He phoned me the following Sunday: 'You spoke too soon – I've got another letter of resignation.'

The Loch Fyne Oyster spell fell on Bob Craig too, a reflection of the way that Andy Lane's vow as a small boy had shaped the company.

I have learned a lot from Loch Fyne Oysters, particularly a respect for the environment and a care for the world, which was maybe missing in me before. I value that.

But Bob Craig did not find it easy to establish formal board procedures into the habitual ways of running the business.

Johnny was basically a salesman – he had a tremendous marketing instinct. What he was not so good at was the nitty-gritty of following things up. Even on the days when everyone would be slicing salmon, he wouldn't be slicing salmon. He was slightly above that, and of course he was running his estate at the same time. He left Andy to get on with the running of the company. That was the way it grew, with the result that Andy tended to get left with every major decision that didn't involve marketing or PR. Andy would say, 'I think we ought to do this,' and if Johnny nodded, that was it agreed. I found it difficult in the early stages that we would solemnly discuss something at a board meeting and I would minute it, and then later I would ask what had happened about it. 'Oh, we decided not to do that,' Andy would say, meaning that *he* had decided not to do it. Johnny would go along with that; he didn't mind as long as it did not cut across the Loch Fyne name and promoting the sale of oysters.

Thus by the early 1990s the company had a stable business, a great name and the beginnings of a governance structure. Amidst the seething mass of activity there was no discernible management structure, but Loch Fyne Oysters was poised for growth.

7. Growth

Many businesses stay small – just a couple of partners, happily working away, supporting the lifestyles with which they are content. However, if a business is to grow, many things are required: practical ideas on how to grow; a system for keeping things under control as growth takes off, changing everything from time to time with random unpredictability; and cash. But above all it needs people. The founders have to find employees who are competent, able to make a contribution, and prepared to do so.

What the founders offer in return is much more than just employment. The people who join the business in the early stages share some of the excitement of building, creating, inventing new things. They share in the dreams and the struggles. They work closely with the founders and often become friends with them. They can feel like real partners in the business, and they can in fact play that role.

But they aren't partners – they are employees. They may play a full part in growing the company, they may help the founders to achieve things that would have been impossible without them; yet they are mere employees, which means that nothing that they help create belongs to them in any way – no part of it is theirs. So when the time comes to sell the business, the founders may walk away with millions, but the employees, who played key roles in helping to build it, get nothing.

★

Great businesses often have small beginnings. In 1950 the first Head Skis were made in the kitchen of the inventor, Howard Head. In 1975 Apple Computer famously started in a garage belonging to the parents of Steve Jobs. Loch Fyne Restaurants, which grew into a company much bigger than Loch Fyne Oysters, its progenitor, can trace its roots back to 1980, to a schoolboy sitting on the wall of the old bridge at the head of Loch Fyne, selling fish out of an open wooden fish-box.

Daniel Sumsion, a nephew of Johnny Noble, was the first to do this, encouraged by his uncle. Passing tourists were intrigued and keen to buy. Andy Lane and David Weir took their turns at selling by the road too. Encouraged by early success, they built a wooden hut at the head of the loch and employed local women to run a shop there. It prospered from the start. The women sold a lot more than the roughly dressed, unshaven men.

One of the young women was Christine MacCallum, married to the shepherd on the Ardkinglas estate, himself the son and grandson of the shepherds before him. She had no experience at all of shop-keeping, but came to love the process of charming even the most difficult customers. She took pride in the growing number of things they sold in the shop: oysters, of course, smoked salmon, fresh and smoked trout and haddock, marinated herring, cockles and mackerel, and tea and coffee. Oysters and tea from a hut by the roadside – the beginning of a great chain of restaurants.

Even children were recruited to serve, wielding sharp knives to open the oysters. There were fewer regulations then. But no one had to work for too long at a time.

Along at the hut there were no toilet facilities, so it was four-hour shifts. You just had to go along and that was it: ten to two and two to six.

Later, in talks with potential investors, this could be presented as a pilot retailing project, which uncovered the market potential of fresh and smoked fish and other products sold to the passing tourist trade, especially by clean-looking young women. With this market study, and in accordance with their long-term strategic business plan, the directors could approve the investment that they had always intended to make: to open a restaurant and a shop.

Actually, it wasn't like that at all. There was no strategic business plan, and no one was thinking of a market study, still less of a restaurant. They were just desperate to sell fish by any means they could. The employees were getting their wages, but the two owners were hardly ever able to take any money out at all, and there was no stability.

By the time of the buyout over twenty years later, Christine MacCallum had become the manager of the shop, selling goods worth the best part of £1m a year. As the business had grown, she had learned in practice how to manage it, without any previous experience or training. (She applied for training once, but was told that she was doing fine.)

Johnny Noble's nephews and nieces loved staying with their unpredictable, incorrigibly subversive, oyster-obsessed uncle. His niece Virginia Sumsion found herself sucked into the business rather more quickly than she had anticipated. She was a student, and agreed to help out at a new initiative, serving at a food stall.

The first Highland Show we did was when Scotland was in the World Cup. Johnny was desperate to go and watch. He left my boyfriend and me to man the stall, having never opened an oyster in our lives. A Frenchwoman took pity on us and showed us how to do it, while Johnny was in the pub watching Scotland lose.

Since then she has attended, with one or two fellow proselytisers, dozens and dozens of food fairs all over the UK, giving up weekends, driving most of the night and sleeping in outlandish places, to spread the name and the products of Loch Fyne Oysters.

You can become quite passionate about it. And you don't have to have been here from the year dot – you see new people coming in and becoming committed quite quickly.

On the operational side – the oyster farm and the salmon smoking and slicing and the logistics to get the orders out – Andy Lane himself was directly in charge, and it was not until 1991 that he recruited David Attwood as manager for that side of the business. Far from moving into his managing role, when he first joined he was pitched into the Christmas rush in the slicing room. He found that it was a good way to get to know Andy Lane.

Andy would just love to get into the guts of the smoke-house ... he'd come and he'd be busy trying to get production up, slicing fish. As the lorry deadline approached his slices would get thicker and thicker and he didn't have the patience to re-lay the slices on the side of salmon, so he'd roll them into a ball and give them to the ladies in the kitchen to re-lay with the interleaving.

The working hours were longer, and the feelings generated were deeper, than in most companies.

There were great times when you would have a sherry or a whisky and production would go on late into the small hours. That's how the company was grown, on these long hours. We also worked one in three weekends, fourteen days on the trot. You did that to get the business established and growing.

One of the earliest to join was Greta Cameron, who became a central figure in the creation of the restaurant business. Small and vital, she came originally from Cairndow farming stock. She was not a trained chef or restaurant manager – she simply had an interest in cooking, which had been fostered by years spent travelling and working in France and cooking freelance in the Channel Islands. Returning with three teenage children to Cairndow after a divorce, she needed money. She first applied to Andy Lane for a position as part-time bookkeeper, and asked for more work when she needed to support the children through college.

Andy said the only thing available was cleaning the smokehouse. I've never forgiven him. Each morning I used to go off up to the smokehouse dressed in oilskins, and clean all the barrels and the floor. Then I'd do the purchase ledger in the afternoon.

Her nose wrinkles at the memory. There are jobs in a fish–processing operation that are not in themselves attractive or satisfying. But her eyes wrinkle too, in a forgiving smile.

Johnny used to bring customers up from London to Ardkinglas House, and that would impress them. But he was never too keen to show them the smokehouse.

The first steps towards what eventually became the Oyster Bar were not part of a grand plan. The impetus came from what was at first a problem for the estate. In 1984 Johnny Noble, as ever in need of cash for the estate, put the old farm buildings at the head of the loch up for sale. When they failed to attract a buyer, the two founders decided to make use of them.

To the visionaries in charge, these were attractive rustic buildings with potential. All the operations could be brought together there. To Greta Cameron and Mary Munro, the office employees who had to move there from the heated outbuilding of the estate house, they were dingy and primitive. In Andy Lane's words:

It was just a big old Dutch barn, with puddles on the floor. And it was bloody cold. The office for me was a place where you could go in your wellies and your flat hat, and it would be a comfortable 10° Centigrade, which wasn't quite what they were looking for.

It wasn't easy to attract *anyone* to work in Loch Fyne Oysters, with the locals thinking it would never succeed. It was important not to demoralise the few brave individuals who were prepared to get involved – even arachnophobes.

On the first day a huge spider abseiled down from the ceiling. I thought Greta and Mary were going to walk out, they were so hacked off.

The smokery was moved into one of the outbuildings, and typically, Johnny Noble persuaded Keith Floyd, the well-known chef, to travel up from the south to make a speech at the opening party. The little hut was closed and the shop established in a corner of the barn, beside the wholesale operations. It wasn't very professional: when somebody came into the shop one of the office workers would jump up from the desk to serve. And it was not unusual to have a visit from a nosy sheep – the yard on the other side of the wall was still used as a sheep pen.

The next stage was slightly, but only slightly, more planned. Customers were buying oysters and smoked salmon from the shop, and sitting around outside to eat them, often in the rain. What about giving them some shelter – a picnic area? Alec Gordon occupied the best farm building on the site. A good friend of both Johnny Noble and Andy Lane, he had moved to Loch Fyne, his favourite fishing area, to rebuild his life after he had honourably paid off all his creditors when his carpet retailing business had gone bust. The old farm building was stacked high with carpets, and Alec Gordon would sit in the middle of them, muffled against the cold, an eternal plume of smoke the only clue to his location. In 1985 he agreed readily to move round the corner, to another of the outhouses. For the first time the customers of Loch Fyne Oysters could have shelter. Andy Lane:

> We became restaurateurs by accident. What we were really trying to do was give people an indoor picnic area so that they could buy stuff in the shop and eat it under cover.

Greta Cameron rose to the challenge. The doorway was hung with 'rustic' sacking to keep the worst of the draughts out, and a big industrial gas blower was installed to take the worst of the edge off the cold. Johnny Noble, always good at making the most of presentation, named it the Loch Fyne Oyster Bar. But she remembers how they were stung at the reaction of the local community.

> It soon spread round the area: 'An Oyster Bar at the head of Loch Fyne? What a joke!'

The scepticism seemed quite reasonable, given the conditions. Andy Lane:

> It was just a bothy. Every time there was a wind the tiles used to chatter together, and tiny chippings would fall on to your soup like pepper. Honestly.

The dishwasher had limited capacity, and at busy times a long queue of dirty dishes snaked round the floor.

It helped that they quickly secured a licence to sell alcohol – unthinkable that an operation run by Johnny Noble would not sell wine – and so the oysters and smoked salmon could be served with a glass chosen from his excellent list of personal favourites.

People kept coming, more and more of them. To meet the demand, newly installed kitchen equipment, usually bought second-hand, had to be mastered by new employees; there was little time for the existing staff to learn the skills themselves, let alone to carry out training. One customer, a medical doctor from Helensburgh, once ordered the Hot Potatoes proudly advertised as 'New!', the first hot dish other than soup, tea and coffee. When they were brought to his table they were cold. So he called over the young waitress, a local girl. With a smile she responded in her lilting Highland voice:

Well, we've just bought the microwave, and I haven't quite got the hang of it. Maybe next time you come I'll be able to work it.

He's still a regular visitor.

Greta Cameron grew into the job of running the picnic area and the kitchen. She had to work without much effective support from the founders. One day Johnny Noble dropped a large pile of plates, and she banned him from helping. Andy Lane, serving soup to help out in a busy period, spilled it over a customer. He was banished back to the shore.

With the wholesale business, the picnic area and the shop all bringing ever-increasing custom, in 1985, after seven years of losses, the company made its first profit.

They soon ran out of space in the kitchen, and over the years repeatedly expanded and reshaped the area. The

Oyster Bar proper (as opposed to the picnic area with that name), which was opened the following year, 1986, also developed over time, taking over larger areas but always retaining the simple wooden furniture and stalls in keeping with the old stone buildings.

As was perhaps always clear to the customers, many of whom began to return again and again, Andy Lane and Johnny Noble were building something different. Andy Lane:

> I suppose the luck was being able to do our own thing, in this part of the world. There was a naivety that helped – the fact that we didn't really know very much, we weren't trained in anything relevant, if anything at all. So we were actually creating a world around us that we liked and that we hoped other people would like. When it came to the restaurant we said, 'Let's open all day, every day, so that you can pop in for a bit of salmon any time,' because that's the kind of place we liked going to, or would have liked to go to. It was in the days when it was still quite intimidating to go to UK restaurants, as they only opened for certain hours, and you were given the whole massed ranks of cutlery, you were never quite sure which fork went with what. Not to mention the cathedral hush, with just the clicking of cutlery. We wanted to be different, we wanted to be the kind of place we'd found abroad. So we did create our own world, in the hope that other people would tune into it. And they did.

One of the discoveries they made overseas was the crab bars in Maryland, near Washington, DC. Johnny Noble was taken there in 1986 by friends and loved the unpretentious approach – very fine food indeed served at any hour on tables covered not by tablecloths but simply by old newspapers. And he once picked the brains of the manager of one of the restaurants in the Red Lobster chain in the United States for over an hour, learning everything he could about every aspect of their business.

It fell to Greta Cameron above all to make it work. With the help of just one other person she did the cooking and organised the restaurant. Their mantra was, 'Keep it simple, don't muck it around.' Everything was to be local Scottish food, not cheap but very good. Johnny Noble was better at cooking than at carrying plates, and worked up many of the recipes himself. Soon he recruited Michel Hedoin as a consultant, who had them adopt a more professional approach, making up manuals of recipes and methods.

Greta Cameron has fond memories of this time. Johnny Noble was always generous with the wine, and the spirit of what was now beginning to be seen as 'the old days' was still very much alive.

> It was good that most nights in the Oyster Bar we used to get together at the end of the day, even if you would often waken up with a massive headache the next morning. Often we used to have brilliant laughs – and good heated debates as well.

Johnny Noble's influence was seen also in other ways.

> Johnny was very easy to get on with. If you had an idea he would listen to you. He was for ever trying everyone's ideas. He never said, 'Oh no, that'll never work,' but

'Let's try it and see how it goes.' And touch wood, most things came right.

Andy Lane too was a generator of ideas, but he was also clearly a boss.

Andy was the MD of the company, so he had to keep people going. He had to keep everything going. If he hadn't kept things going we wouldn't be here today. He maybe had less patience than Johnny. If something had to be done and he wanted it done then you had to do it, and you respected that, because he had very, very good ideas. Even if it wasn't right, you would still do it, and then he would realise afterwards, and he would apologise. That was a good thing – we could all apologise.

For all of them, Loch Fyne Oysters was the main focus of their lives. None of the three was married – and it was just as well, noted Greta Cameron.

I don't think Andy and Johnny had time to marry. Even me, to be honest, I couldn't have done what I did if I'd been married. Not the hours. For everybody it was seven days a week, and twelve hours a day. I was more than once divorced, and the children were older, so I could do that. Then we had to watch, because when we started employing more people we were expecting them to do that as well. So we had to pull back and say, 'Look, other people can't do this. We've done it because we're not married.' I think there's a lot of that in it.

Johnny Noble and Andy Lane together were a brilliant entrepreneurial pair, driven by boundless energy and complete concentration, and fizzing with new ideas. Consequently, in 1990 Greta Cameron found herself in Nottingham, opening the first of what became a whole series of Loch Fyne Restaurants modelled on the original Oyster Bar.

She puts the expansion down to the founders' desire to be recognised.

> Both of them wanted to try and prove to people that it worked, that it wasn't a kind of joke, that it would also work in cities.

In 1983 the first attempt at starting something away from the base at Loch Fyne had been a painful learning experience. Andy Lane is rueful.

> We'd proved that this could work here, and it was always Johnny's vision that we would also do it elsewhere. I thought, 'Great, we've got a wooden shack here that's coining it, let's do one in Edinburgh'. So we set up a shop in William Street. But it was another thing altogether to drive off at four o'clock in the morning, in a van half full of our produce, going via the fish market in Glasgow to stock up with white fish from the east coast. It was an absolutely bloody nightmare. And it didn't work. It was in the wrong place, in William Street – much too quiet. We had a queue of people, but they were all ladies of a certain age from Morningside who were buying bits of whiting for their cats for 50p a time. 'I don't eat fish myself!' Oh God!

So I was a bit jaundiced, but Johnny felt we could do
a franchise, and it was his energy that got the restaurants
off the ground.

The choice of site was not based on measures of population and buying power, social class and frequency of
eating out: the decisive factor was that a number of Andy
Lane's family lived in the vicinity of Nottingham. His
relatives knew the area and would help out, and provide
beds for the people from Loch Fyne.

The proximity of the cricket ground at Trent Bridge
may also have had an influence on the siting of the restaurant. This was not because cricket supporters were
expected to be large purchasers of shellfish, but because
Andy Lane loved cricket, and many subsequent visits
to the Nottingham restaurant coincided with important
matches. So it is that many a corporate HQ has been
moved, ostensibly for good business reasons, to a city
beloved of the chief executive. Little is ever heard of
cricket in the west of Scotland: in the pursuit of building
his business a devoted entrepreneur may postpone not
only his marriage prospects but even his favourite sport.
It was not until 1998 that Andy finally achieved his dream
of marrying, but now perhaps he would at least be able
to enjoy some cricket.

With the painful experience of Edinburgh ever present,
the run-up to the opening of the Nottingham restaurant
was an anxious period. Greta Cameron and Andy Lane
spent a great deal of time in Nottingham. Johnny Noble
organised the opening party, aimed at making the largest
possible impact in the local area, as well as more widely
on the restaurant trade. But as opening day approached,

the tension became too much for Andy Lane; he disappeared, and could not be contacted. The day after the
opening he phoned, to be reassured by Greta Cameron
that from the first there had been a queue out of the door.
The restaurant was successful from day one.

However, the personal cost to the people responsible
was considerable. Andy Lane:

> It was Greta and I that ended up running the restaurants.
> I'm not a restaurateur – I wanted to be an oyster farmer
> and wear welly boots all the time. But we ended up
> driving up and down the motorway.

For Greta Cameron it was a huge commitment away
from home.

> It took a lot of strength to run it from here. I would go
> down on a Monday morning and probably drive back on
> a Friday evening.

Two years later they opened the second restaurant,
in Elton, near Peterborough. Andy Lane's brother Martin
helped find, buy and prepare the barn in which it is
sited. After leaving the RAF at the age of thirty-eight
he had done well buying old cottages, doing them up
and selling them, until the recession of 1991 wiped out
his business. The Elton property, a fairly well-known
landmark only 5 miles from Oundle, near where Andy
and Martin had lived as boys, was a very fine set of
farm buildings, nearly 200 years old, with cobbled court-
yards and crests over the doors. Martin Lane carried
out an amazingly low-cost conversion, and up until the

time of writing no further alterations have had to be made.

Again under Greta Cameron's leadership, it was a success from the first, and again it increased the pressure on the people involved.

They might not have been able to do it if they had been married, but Andy Lane still dreamed of having a family. In the midst of all these pressures, he was attending Buddhist meditation retreats regularly, something he found valuable and relaxing. In 1994, at the age of forty-three, he met Liz Wright at a retreat centre in the countryside near Balquhidder. At thirty-three, she was Deputy Director of the MacRobert Arts Centre in Stirling. They took to each other easily and naturally, and arranged a first date in Stirling not long afterwards. They discovered among other things a common interest in the wildness of nature, and shared childhood dreams of living in remote country areas, surrounded by animals.

She introduced him to the world of the arts, in which to her relief he took great delight, and they shared expeditions around Loch Fyne, the surrounding hills and further afield. Four years later he proposed on the island of Torsa during a sailing trip on Bob Craig's yacht. Their Highland wedding was attended with wild celebrations by many of their friends among the long-serving Loch Fyne Oysters people. In the following year the dream was completed by the birth of their first son.

Taking stock of the restaurants in 1997, the two entrepreneurs realised that they would have to recruit professional restaurateurs to help. A head-hunter put up two candidates, the first being Ian Glyn. They liked him so much that they did not bother even to interview the second.

Ian Glyn's main expertise was in finding and buying good sites for restaurants. His business partner Mark Derry had run restaurant chains with great success. For Whitbread, the brewing company, he had developed new ways of branding and running restaurants, and had been a member of the small team that turned round the pub chain 'Thank God It's Friday' – 'TGIF' – from a loss of £1m a year to a profit of the same amount. Given an unsympathetic boss, Mark Derry left, negotiating a good payout on the way. With three friends he bought a small quoted company and used it to acquire from Ian Glyn a small chain of pub-restaurants. They built them up for a few years and then sold them. With mad cow disease in the headlines they began to look at fish restaurants. And by good fortune it was just then that the Loch Fyne Oysters' head-hunter rang up.

Johnny Noble's message was simple: let's do this together, with all four – Johnny Noble and Andy Lane, Mark Derry and Ian Glyn – sharing ownership equally. Bob Craig, the accountant-director who acted so often as a deal-maker for the two principals in Loch Fyne Oysters, came into his own in the negotiations. At the meeting to thrash out the heads of terms, which formed the basis for what became a lasting and fruitful partnership, Mark Derry suggested that they would need £1m in capital, to provide the necessary funds for opening a series of new restaurants. After some reflection, Johnny Noble thought he could raise half of that. Ian Glyn said that it was one of his principles never to ask a friend to invest in one of his business ventures. But he and Mark Derry agreed that they should be able to raise the other half.

Ian Glyn and Mark Derry saw the potential strength of the Loch Fyne Oysters brand and were attracted by the prospect of control over the supply of fish, which tended to suffer from fluctuating availability and prices. Andy Lane and his colleagues in Loch Fyne Oysters were experts. Working with them would be a genuine advantage to anyone opening a fish restaurant.

At the end of the meeting, Bob Craig remembers, Mark Derry said, 'Hmm, there is just one thing . . .' When he had left Whitbread he had promised his partner that they would go travelling together for perhaps a year. She had resigned from her job and was all set to head abroad with him. If he decided to stay and join the new venture instead, that was fine with her, but she was going travelling anyway. Mark Derry was therefore going abroad. An anthropologist might call that 'mate-guarding', and it proved a good decision: an enduring marriage followed.

On 1 January 1998 the new company took over the two restaurants at Nottingham and Elton. The style of the restaurants they intended to open would, like these two, reflect the original Oyster Bar on Loch Fyne – simple wooden furniture, high-quality food, as far as possible brought in from local and impeccably sustainable sources, the whole a celebration of the beauty and natural purity of the oceans at their best.

With Mark Derry unavoidably away, Johnny raised virtually the full £1m needed to fund the additional growth they were aiming at. The four founders had paid £1 per share for their initial 50,000 shares each; the plan they then produced gave sufficient confidence to raise the additional money at £2.50 per share. It took more than a year, most of the money coming from Johnny Noble's friends and contacts from Eton.

Ian Glyn spent the year identifying possible new sites, clearing the way for rapid growth after the expected launch. He needed to keep in touch with Mark Derry in South America – what started as an occasional correspondence turned by the end of the year into three phone calls a week. The first opening by the new company was to be in 1999 in Cambridge, on a much bigger site than the two existing ones. Mark Derry arrived back and the following day went straight to Cambridge: he didn't like the site, worried that it was in the wrong place. They had bought a pub with no parking, and its sales were only £3000 a week – nothing like enough to run a restaurant. But when it opened, the first week's turnover was over nine times that figure, about four times the average of the other two restaurants. It never flagged.

As so often, the detail of how this actually happened is far from what is taught in business schools, or told with hindsight in case studies. Mark Derry:

> The day before it opened we painted the bar ourselves. It was a big rush, and it was a long way from perfect. At the opening, the first person I spoke to was vegetarian – 'I'm sorry, I don't eat fish.' It was only then that I realised we didn't have anything for veggies. We hadn't thought about it, so it was just green beans. It was pathetic. And the training was appalling. I had come from a background of really top-quality restaurants, where we would spend £150,000 training people before we opened, just on one restaurant. But we did it on a shoestring, expecting two

days beforehand to get everybody in. And nobody turned up. We'd done all these interviews and thought that would be all right, and we had four people turn up. So we were frantically going round other bars and chatting people up to come and work there. My first cup of tea had a tea bag floating in it. It was dreadful. But people persevered, because they loved the kind of innocent nature of it all, and people took to it and it just rocked.

The same magic that had kept Andy Lane working all day every day for a pittance, and Johnny Noble travelling the world indefatigably talking about oysters, and Greta Cameron cleaning the smokery and travelling the motorways to run restaurants, and Christine MacCallum charming even the most difficult customers in the shop, and the two Davids working and driving and drinking as if they were heroes from Homer – this same magic now appeared in Cambridge. Mark Derry, looking back, recognises that there is something in the spirit of Loch Fyne Oysters that is captivating, and it was largely inspired by Johnny Noble.

Ian and I started this together with Bob and Johnny and Andy, and it was wildly eccentric. Given that I am a much more straightforward kind of operator – you know, this is what I do – it was interesting to get involved in something which had such a lot of history and an incredible amount of energy. I mean, Johnny was just extraordinary: larger than life, an enormous character, full of energy, and he drank furiously into the wee hours of the morning. Not many people had said 'No!' to him in his life – he was not used to any form of tempering.

One of the eccentricities was the way that Johnny Noble would deal with complaints.

He was fiercely protective. A woman wrote to him from Nottingham and ended with something along the lines of, 'I'll never darken your door again!' He wrote in reply, 'It is with enormous relief that we note you will not be returning to our restaurant.' There were a couple of these in the early days, so I said, 'Don't you think it would be better if I deal with the complaints, Johnny?' Because he was basically telling people to sod off.

Liz Long, running the home delivery sales, remembers similar treatment being given to an elderly gentleman, a regular customer in France.

He used to fax his orders through, and on this one occasion he sent a strong letter of complaint about the produce he'd received. I tried to appease him without success, so I asked Johnny to have a go. He tried to be pleasant, also without success. So he sent a fax saying, 'I, sir, choose to be obnoxious. You clearly cannot help it.' We didn't hear from him again.

But the customers kept coming, and soon more restaurants were opened, and again did well from the outset. Their customers were not young. Mark Derry:

The average age was staggeringly old – every time a hearse went by we had lost another customer. Ironically the average age drops the longer we're open: I think what happens is they bring their kids who are around forty, and it then tumbles through the generations. Oysters and smoked salmon weren't naturally youngsters' products, but I think it's having a renaissance with the young due to the move towards sustainable, healthy eating.

There is no single reason for the success.

We have endless debates. Is it the brand? Is it the location? Is it the operation? Or what? But the whole works together really well.

8. Death

To many people Johnny Noble *was* Loch Fyne Oysters. Wherever he had travelled on the company's business – visiting restaurants in London, grand hotels in Hong Kong, distributors in New York – it was the memory of meeting Johnny Noble that kept a special aura around the company name.

No one doubted his devotion to the whole enterprise. But despite appearances, he and Loch Fyne Oysters were separate. For him the appeal of the proposal to start the company had included its potential to provide income for the people on the estate, but also, and mainly, its potential eventually to relieve him of the burden of inherited debt. Bob Craig, the outside director, put it like this:

> Johnny made it quite clear from the outset that his first priority was Ardkinglas House, and that Loch Fyne Oysters, while he prized it very highly, was secondary. One day he would have to cash in his chips, to leave his estate in good heart for the next person coming along.

Johnny Noble's main ambition was not to burden the next generation with the ordeal that he himself had faced when his father died. He had only briefly considered selling the company to its managers, and had not pursued the idea, partly for fear of having to accept a relatively low price for the shares. Despite appearances he was not well off – he needed to get every penny he could if the estate was going to be secure. With his holding in Loch Fyne Restaurants, he did not depend totally on the prospect of selling his shares in Loch Fyne Oysters. But he could not afford to be generous.

For some years, together with Andy Lane and Bob Craig he had talked informally with his cousin Tim Noble, who ran a successful merchant bank in Edinburgh, about cashing in the shares – selling the company. Tim Noble had all the necessary expertise in valuing, marketing and selling companies. In autumn 2001 Johnny Noble finally decided to get everybody together formally. There seemed to be no rush, so the meeting was fixed for February 2002.

Meanwhile, Johnny Noble was not well. It was not in his character to share his troubles, whether in finance or health; of those around him, few were aware that he had diabetes, which he had always carried off nonchalantly, as if it was nothing. They were all vividly conscious of the amount he drank, which, because it never seemed to blunt his capabilities, was a matter of wonder rather than concern.

It was entirely in character that he made no one aware of his worsening illness. So it was all the more of a shock when one autumn day in 2001, after breakfast in the Oyster Bar and as usual following it with his first glass of 'pop' of the day, he collapsed on to the floor. This had never happened before. Unable to get up, he was still on the floor when the local doctor, a long-standing friend, arrived. The doctor checked him over and, with a bedside manner only appropriate in a very concerned friend, berated him for neglecting his health and for his drinking.

'OK, OK, doctor!' His voice was weak. 'I surrender!'

But he didn't. How could living be counted as living, without a flow of 'pop'?

A few months later, towards the end of the year, in a meeting with the Loch Fyne Restaurants people, he was taken ill again. The diagnosis was liver cancer.

Over the next few weeks, Johnny Noble deteriorated visibly. He still came into the Oyster Bar, and the people working there were appalled to watch the slide. This man had all his life, by sheer exuberance, single-handedly brought to life the great empty house at the head of the loch; had inspired with his energy and bonhomie group after group of visitors to become loyal customers; and had thrown party after party for all the employees to anoint each newly installed piece of kitchen equipment. Now he was shrinking before their eyes. Gaunt and haggard on what turned out to be his last visit in January 2002, he had to be helped into his car and driven home.

Soon afterwards he called Andy Lane and Bob Craig to Ardkinglas. When they arrived, they found that he had dragged himself out of bed, dressed, and was waiting in the great drawing room overlooking the loch. The visitors were aware of the extraordinary courage it must have taken for him to get there, but these three very different characters had in common a certain reserve, and it was not overtly acknowledged. They asked about his health, and he gave little away in his reply. His voice, which had always boomed even when he whispered, was weak.

'Well,' said Andy Lane, 'I'm going to hope for the best.'

He will always remember the long, kindly look that Johnny Noble gave him, saying nothing.

Then they turned to the point of the gathering.

'Go ahead with the meeting with Tim next week, boys.' Johnny Noble paused for breath. 'Keep talking to him.' Another pause. 'Something will turn up.'

Something will turn up. For Bob Craig and Andy Lane, looking back, those words carried a prophetic charge.

Two days later, on 3 February 2002, Johnny Noble died.

Andy Lane felt it as much as anyone, but his expression of loss is understated, like the emotion that must have filled the drawing room at their last meeting.

What a gap. That huge character, stalwart and inspirational. Gone. Like Ben Nevis not being there.

9. Predators

After Johnny Noble's death, loss suffused and quietened Loch Fyne Oysters, weighing down with a sense of absence the people who had worked with him. Occasionally they were ambushed by grief – coming round the corner from the kitchen and seeing the table where he had so often sat, or driving along the bumpy track to the oyster-processing sheds, past Ardkinglas House, now even from a distance ringing with emptiness. Ritual phrases – that he had had a good innings and that at least it had been pretty quick – failed utterly to counteract their sorrow. But the show had to go on, and for a while everyone worked quietly, without arguments, their smiles tinged with sadness.

The village filled with quiet chatter, breeding rumours that provided no reassurance. Like the gutter press, the grapevine feeds on the sensational and the threatening. Johnny Noble's death was imbued with both.

Did you hear how he collapsed in the restaurant? And what about the drink? Who will be chairman now? Will it be sold? It could just collapse!

The gossips were eager for pain and for failure, so that they could shake their heads and be sympathetic and wise.

The show did go on. As usual, people came and ate in the restaurant and spent more in the shop than they had planned. Most of them didn't know about Johnny Noble – inconceivably, it seemed, for how could one not sense the huge emotional crater at the head of the loch? Some did know and were sympathetic, which was worse. There was as always a duty to be briskly cheerful with them all.

Underneath, uncertainty gradually spread its chill tentacles, fed by the questions on the village grapevine. What would happen now? The long-serving knew that as well as having almost single-handedly built the brand, Johnny Noble had owned a controlling stake, more than half the shares. Most only knew vaguely what that meant, but everyone could feel that it was ominous. Insecurity spread like a monstrous, bloodsucking plant that got everywhere, lying in wait, triggering fear.

Andy Lane and Bob Craig did their best to preserve a sense of normality. But nothing was normal. The meeting with Tim Noble now had a sense of urgency that had never been there before. Its purpose was no longer to plan for something that might happen in some vague future – it was to solve an urgent, major problem.

Johnny Noble's will was in good order and was resolved in three months. He had achieved what he had always aimed at, passing on a dream instead of the nightmare of his own inheritance. The estate and its imposing house, together with the shares in Loch Fyne Oysters, went to David Sumsion, his nephew.

At Andy Lane's invitation, Bob Craig became chairman, a move that had been anticipated on the shop floor and was readily accepted by the others. Soon he received a phone call from an Edinburgh lawyer acting for 'the majority shareholder', with an instruction to postpone any meetings aimed at selling the company.

Bob Craig, however, knew the detail of the company's legal documents. Years earlier, when Andy Lane had passed over the controlling stake to Johnny Noble, they agreed that if Johnny Noble died first, his shares would automatically lose their voting rights. The board, which had expanded by now to include some of the senior managers, would then choose when to restore the votes. This ensured that Andy Lane would not be left powerless with a minority stake while someone new came in with the right to make all the decisions – exactly the current situation had it not been for this provision. So although it was fully accepted that David Sumsion now owned more than half the shares and they had to take account of his interests, for the time being he did not have any voting rights. Of course he would be consulted and they were anxious to take his views into account, but he would have to wait until a conclusion that was satisfactory all round had been reached before he got voting rights on his shares.

As had been urged by Johnny Noble at that last meeting, they now commissioned Tim Noble to sell the company. The fee agreed included a significant bonus if a price of more than £4m was achieved – but the basic fee seemed huge anyway. The first step was to prepare a prospectus that Tim Noble would circulate. Given the fee arrangements, it was a surprise that most of the work actually seemed to be done by the people in Loch Fyne Oysters. It took weeks of concentrated effort. Andy Lane kept the managers informed of what was going on, but there was no way of stopping the rumour mill that filled everyone with misgivings.

A few weeks later small groups of men in dark suits started to appear from time to time. Helped by David

Attwood, soon to be appointed to the board as operations
director, Andy Lane would show them round with a
permanent sinking feeling in his gut. Never sartorially
fastidious, he now dressed down even further, his thread-
bare jeans, climbing boots and ancient pullover a mute
personal protest at the procession of suits.

The staff were well aware of the reason for these unusual visits, although nothing was officially said to them.
Some of the visitors seemed quite genuine, reasonable
people. Others seemed cold and distant. Some were
knowledgeable, others less so. Tension rose perceptibly,
although most of the staff were outwardly philosophical.
There was nothing they could do about it but hope for
the best.

Andy Lane, on the other hand, was in a position to do
something about it, and it preyed on his mind. Until
recently he had never seen the company as potentially
very valuable, and he was amazed to find that his shares
might be worth £1m or more. But he worried about the
employees, now numbering more than 100. *He* would be
all right – but what about them? After years of working
together with the people who had done so much to build
the business, and who had shared with him unforgettable
moments of desperation, hilarity and triumph, could he
just sell his shares and abandon them?

Recognising the huge efforts that the managers had
made, the two owners had given share options to eight
of them, so they would each get a sum of cash when the
company was sold. But it would be a small sum compared
to Andy Lane's and David Sumsion's, and small compensation for the fact that of all the employees these eight
would be the most likely to lose their jobs.

David Attwood, helping to show round people who might be his bosses in a month or two, wanted to give them a good impression of himself as well as of the company. Christine MacCallum also felt insecure, having had no experience other than in this one company, and no wider training. How would that look to the new owners, whoever they might turn out to be?

Greta Cameron, running the restaurant, was acutely aware of Andy Lane's dilemma.

> Andy's very sensitive. He was responsible for a lot of staff and he used to worry about them. The last thing he would have wanted would have been to get a big payment himself and then have to say, 'Sorry, your jobs have gone.' I think that would have cracked him up completely.

The mutual commitment that had grown through the years was only tacit, the affection unspoken. But for the people who had worked with him to build his beloved company, Andy Lane felt something that was close to love. To sell them out would be rank betrayal.

When a company is taken over, those who work there do not usually enjoy the experience. Nothing brings home more starkly the fact that they have no influence over any decision, not even the right to be told anything. They will be the last to discover what has happened, which nonetheless might convulse their lives.

They are plunged into uncertainty, powerless and under threat. One thing they know for sure is that when the takeover is completed, they will be in danger. New managers will almost certainly be appointed over them.

Will they get on with them? One of the managers' tasks will be to get as much cash as possible out of the company for the acquirer, so that the purchase price can be recovered. Anything which can profitably be closed down is closed down; any people who can be 'released' are made redundant.

In the case of Loch Fyne Oysters it was clear to the managers that all the accounting and secretarial work, the sales jobs, the food processing and most of the management would be vulnerable. The most likely acquirers were the owners of a food-processing company, who would move those functions to their existing plants. Even the oyster and mussel farm might be closed: the new owners would discover that it had lost money in several recent years, due to the vagaries of warm weather affecting water quality, so that to preserve absolute purity the shellfish could sometimes not be sold for weeks at a time. What would be left would be a husk, just the Oyster Bar and the shop. The animating spirit would have disappeared: no more links with the local boats, fishing with sustainable methods, no more connection with the communities along the shore. Just an empty brand, the soul and the guts of it gone.

Facing this prospect, quite soon after Johnny Noble's death Andy Lane had mused with Peter Page, a visiting friend, whether they might conceivably manage to 'do a John Lewis'. John Lewis had been partially owned since 1929, and wholly owned since 1951, by a trust for its employees, now over 60,000 in number. It was without doubt the most consistently successful UK retailer. From time to time particular competitors might catch the eye more, but they would all bite the dust or at least run into trouble, while John Lewis continued to do well year after year. Marks and Spencer generally had slightly better recognition on the high street and had sustained that for many years, but even they had recently fallen from their pedestal. One difference between the two was that Marks and Spencer, owned by outside shareholders, were paternalistic in their approach to their employees, whereas John Lewis, owned by the employees' trust, set out consciously and consistently to engage the people working there. There were no 'employees' in John Lewis, only 'partners', and the managers tried hard to make the fact of partnership real to them. Another difference was that the John Lewis partners all shared in the profits they made. The bonus was the same percentage of earnings for everyone in the company – sometimes as high as three months' salary. This bonus was not the result of a group of senior people deciding to provide an incentive, to manipulate the employees into greater effort; it was sharing the fruits of success, fairly, in the business they all owned and were making successful together, as partners. The feelings and the levels of commitment generated by the two systems were very different. Who would not feel happier and work harder as a partner?

A study by economists from the London School of Economics in the early 1990s had shown that in the UK retail trade John Lewis had the highest marginal productivity of labour – perhaps not a surprise, given these policies – but also the highest marginal productivity of capital.[2] That also makes sense. If, for example, a retailer invests in a new computerised till system, it is up to the people who use the system to get it to work effectively. In John Lewis the shop workers are involved from the first as a matter of course; when new equipment is to be installed their views are taken into account even when the initial layout is being designed. This tends to result in better, more practical solutions, and in addition, when the system appears it already feels to the workers as if it is their own. In most retailers, the system would be designed by 'experts' and the people on the shop floor would have little or nothing to do with it until it appeared – as a result they would feel it had been imposed on them, and sometimes it would in fact be poorly designed. Treating people as partners leads to better planning and implementation of capital projects – and John Lewis has the highest marginal capital productivity in the retail trade.

In the LSE study a large company in the highly competitive retail sector had been shown to have the highest productivity of both labour and capital, probably at least in part because of its employee-ownership. One would have expected this to attract some attention. Economists, government ministers and financial journalists all claim that productivity is the Holy Grail. But it passed virtually without comment. It didn't fit the dominant paradigm in economics and in City journalism, which maintained that in order to foster really productive business, what is known as 'capital market discipline' is necessary. The basic idea here is that each company should be owned by *outside* shareholders – not the employees – so that they can punish the company if the top managers do not make it achieve good financial returns. The shareholders (the 'capital market') 'discipline' the company by selling shares, so that the share price falls. If the price falls low enough, the company will be taken over, the top managers sacked and new managers installed to turn the performance round.

This is how they believe that productivity can be achieved. Since John Lewis was not owned by outsiders, and therefore could not be subject to 'capital market discipline', patently its high productivity of both capital and labour must be an aberration, a special case, to be explained away rather than learned from.

There was no conspiracy. The study just remained invisible because it did not fit the dominant model. If established academic authorities acknowledged it they would risk losing face; if merchant bankers did so they might lose the justification for charging huge fees.

Andy Lane, desperate not to sell out the people who had worked with such commitment to build the company, wanted to find a solution that could foster in Loch Fyne Oysters an approach similar to that of John Lewis. But as well as the problem of whether they would get the best price for the company, there seemed to be no way of doing so without people getting into debt – they would each have to borrow a small fortune to pay for the company.

> I'd been banging on to Johnny about John Lewis. He was sympathetic, but he kept coming back to this: the only way to do that was for everyone to get into a whole lot of personal debt. So it would be better to find a secure home.

In November 2002 Andy Lane received a phone call from Peter Page. He had come across an article in the *Financial Times* describing a fund, Baxi Partnership, that helped structure and finance 'management-led, all-employee buyouts'. He would put it in the post.

'Who knows?' he said, 'You may be able to do a John Lewis after all.'

Andy Lane knew that the bids were beginning to come in. He had to move fast. He dared not let hope take root, but for the first time in months hope seemed possible.

10. 'Can You Help?'

On Monday, 9 December 2002 I took a day off to get ahead with my Christmas shopping and was rushing around trying to do it in a day. Everyone else in town seemed to have had the same thought.

My mobile rang.

'Is that David Erdal?' An unassuming, educated English voice.

'Yes.'

'This is Andy Lane, MD of Loch Fyne Oysters. I'm looking at an article in the *Financial Times* about your fund and thought you might be able to help us.'

I took refuge in a doorway from the mass of scurrying shoppers.

'Sounds interesting. Fire away.'

In a few sentences he gave me the bones of the story. He said it would break his heart to see the company sold to a big corporation; he would much rather sell to the employees. I could hear that he was genuine, that he was really interested. He was desperate to avoid letting down the employees.

It was exactly these feelings that in 1983 inspired Philip Baxendale and his cousin Joan Caselton to give 90 per cent of all they owned to found the Baxi Partnership trust. The trust's original purpose was to provide a stable employee-ownership system for their gas boiler-manufacturing company. Now it was aimed at doing the same for others – helping people like the employees of Loch Fyne Oysters win ownership of their company, rather than seeing it sold or closed down. A long and bumpy trajectory had led to my being the MD of the fund, and for me there could be no better job in the world.

Our mantra consisted of three key ideas: 'strong businesses, in employee-ownership, with partnership cultures'. To be strong, businesses had to be well managed, with good strategies. Partnership cultures meant that everyone was informed and involved as a real partner, consulted in decisions, exercising the vote on ownership issues and sharing the rewards. Employee-ownership was the key to making it all genuine. Normally employees might receive information, get involved, have some influence and share in any profit, but it would always be through the goodwill – and good sense – of the managers. Only as owners would the employees share in these important things as of right.

Employee-ownership is good for people and good for business. It makes companies do better, it leads to people having a better understanding of the business they work in, it gives them a say in what they do and it spreads wealth widely. It puts people in charge of their own destinies and makes them richer, each person sharing in any profits made, and over the years building up a personal block of capital.[3]

Owning shares worth even a few thousand pounds makes a real difference. It can give you a deposit on a new car or a house; if you want to set up your own business it can give you a start; and in the event of redundancy it means you have something to fall back on as you look for your next job.

Employee-ownership is not just about getting richer in the sense of getting more money. It is also about being, and being treated as, a full partner in the company, a real player, not simply a passive servant of other people's interests. This builds among the participants understanding and skills that are of use not only inside the company, but also within the community in which they live. It also tends to make people feel better, both about themselves and about what they do.

In 1992, following a long business crisis for Algoma Steel, the third largest steel-maker in Canada, the trade union leaders led the employees in buying control of the company – 60 per cent of the shares – in exchange for a reduction in pay. Those shares were held in cooperative trusts. The union also negotiated a new joint decision-making process giving the workers an equal say in decision-making, from the board of directors to the shop floor. They all then faced the task of making it succeed. That meant getting involved not just as employees, whose sole responsibility was to do what they were told and do it well, but as joint owners, understanding the business and taking responsibility for making it successful.

In order to do that, all of them, managers and employees alike, had to develop new skills and new ways of doing things. Managers had to listen and consult, and be prepared to have their views questioned in public, sometimes robustly. The employees had to learn to participate, to express their views to groups of people, to listen to others even when they did not agree with them, even to make presentations, something many found terrifying at first.

An unforeseen consequence was that they also started to play more of a role in their communities outside work. For example, as their confidence and experience grew, employees who were football supporters began to volunteer to go on the committees of their football clubs, instead of just attending the matches. The same skills proved useful there too.[4]

There is a growing body of 'locus of control' psychological research showing that your health improves if you see yourself as being in charge of your own destiny. For example, people recovering from strokes do better if they believe that they themselves can affect the outcome; people who see themselves as subject to forces outside their control do worse.[5] When you work in a company where you, along with all your co-workers, own the company, and where the managers treat you as a fellow-owner, a full participant whose views are worth listening to and who plays an active part in making things better, you realise through your day-to-day experience that the 'locus of control' really does lie in you. What happens really is to a great extent in your hands. You see it that way because it *is* that way.

Another effect that is good for you, making you happier, is that you experience the company, and its figures of authority, as being on your side. (Managers can easily destroy that perception, if they attempt to exercise their authority rather than involving you as a partner.) As long as the company's aim is clearly *not* to serve your interests, but to make use of you to serve the interests of other people – the fat cats who own it – it is hard to think of the company as being on your side. In fact it would be a bit crazy to try to see it that way. The company is *not* on your side. But the company is one of the main institutions in your life; you spend a very large proportion of your waking hours there. It is not the greatest good fortune to have as your main social environment a place where you are treated not as a fully autonomous person, a partner in the enterprise, but as a servant, whose motives may be suspect and who has to be supervised and 'incentivised', who may easily become a cost to be got rid of rather than a contributor worth listening to. It doesn't encourage a sense that you can make a difference. And no matter how much particular managers and companies try to prettify the relationship, with employee benefits and involvement schemes, with corporate social responsibility programmes and charitable donations, the underlying fact lies in wait to accost you in a crisis: the company where you work is using you for the benefit of its owners. When the crunch comes, your interests are last on the list.

Research I carried out in a prosperous part of northern Italy suggests that this may have a wide impact. I compared the populations of three towns where the proportion of people working in companies owned and controlled by their employees varied from 0 per cent to 26 per cent. In the town with no employee-owned companies the people were less trustful of the local political authorities – they saw them as being less strongly on their side. And their children did worse at school, playing truant more and achieving lower grades. It is possible that those accustomed to being owners are not only more active in local activities, but also more positive about *all* the institutions they meet. This attitude rubs off on to their children. No matter how much children may want an education, their school is an institution. If the parents experience the company where they work as a benign institution in which they play a real part, the children will tend to see their school in the same light. They are less inclined to play truant.

One amazing discovery was that in the town with the highest proportion of employment in companies owned by their employees, the people actually lived significantly longer. This fits with a growing body of evidence suggesting that being placed low in a hierarchy is bad for people – it actually makes them die at an earlier age.[6]

This may be partly to do with the good effects of seeing themselves as being in control. It is likely also to owe something to the fact that when the people own the company where they work, the wealth they create together is spread widely among them. It remains local, and feeds into the community in many ways. The gap between rich and poor is thereby reduced – not by taking money from the rich through taxes, but as a built-in stream of cash being delivered naturally to all who help create it. Living in a town where the gap between rich and poor is insultingly visible heightens tension all round. Once the wealth is spread, in a natural way, tension relaxes.[7]

Perhaps this is instinctively insightful and life-preserving – one of the effects associated with a larger gap between rich and poor is a higher homicide rate.[8]

Governments attract considerable resistance when they attempt, through taxing the rich, to make the spread of wealth more even. It is claimed that such policies reduce the incentive to create wealth in the first place.

Whether or not that is true, no government in the developed economies has found an effective way of countering the long-term trend towards an increasing gap between rich and poor.[9] However, this desirable spread of wealth is achieved quite naturally through employee-ownership, simply by sharing the wealth created among those who create it. And far from being a disincentive, this creates a strong shared incentive to work together to create more wealth. Even low levels of share-ownership among employees are associated with strongly improved productivity.

The financial perspective is not the only one that leads Baxi Partnership to help people achieve buyouts of the companies where they work. Yes, this will make everyone richer. But the fact that over time it will also achieve a different quality of life, both personal and social, is equally important. Having good reason to develop a better understanding; greater participation in our lives at work and in the circles we move in outside work; being in control of our lives; seeing other institutions in a more favourable light – all these things are worth achieving in themselves. The reduction in the gap between rich and poor, which leads to a greater sense of community, likewise changes the landscape of our lives: in areas with greater equality people tend to have longer, healthier lives, and the murder rates tend to be lower. Achieving all these things while at the same time helping the companies to become more productive makes this very valuable in human as well as economic terms – a society better than anything yet seen. The purpose of Baxi Partnership is not to maximise profit for itself. Making a profit is necessary to allow the fund to continue, but the purpose that drives the fund is the

vision of productive, satisfying working lives and transformed relationships: a better way of living.

There are certain criteria that companies have to meet
before Baxi Partnership can get involved.

'How many people are employed?' I asked Andy Lane.
At that time our minimum was forty, because below that
a company is usually too dependent on just one person.
That person is usually the owner-entrepreneur, who has
thought of the idea behind the business and made it work,
and who is probably the only person with an overall
concept of the company, together with the confidence to
change things and to start new things. Most owners think
that they will always be like that, as committed as ever,
but in practice, once they have sold most or all of their
shares, their motivation changes. There is nothing like a
huge bank balance to make someone relax. They start
looking around them, finding other things to do with
their time: the villa in Spain or the yacht in the Mediter-
ranean or sometimes starting another business. Probably
a whole team of people will keep their original business
going, so to be successful an employee-buyout needs a
group of competent managers. Baxi Partnership sets a
minimum of forty employees in the expectation that at
that size there will be other capable managers, in addition
to the owner.

Beyond the problem of who will keep the company
going is who in the business is going to pick up the
founder's inventive, driving role. That is a question that
can only be answered over time.

'We're at about 110 employees at the moment.'

First hurdle cleared.

'And is the company profitable?'

Given that the company itself pays the price to the person who sells it, it has to be a strong performer with good profits and not much debt. Otherwise it simply cannot afford to pay out the vendor. It has to borrow all the money, so it has to be able to pay high levels of interest and still generate enough cash to repay the borrowings. This type of deal, known as a 'highly lever- aged buyout', became widely used only in the 1980s. It involves companies taking on levels of debt that would previously have been viewed as reckless, but it works, and it works particularly well when the ownership is shared among all the employees. Many an employee-owned company has weathered storms that would have put a conventionally structured company out of business. But to start with, it has to be profitable, with the capacity to borrow.

'Yes, we made half a million pounds last year, and it's been growing for years. It should keep growing.'

Perfect. We arranged to meet at Loch Fyne Oysters' restaurant in early January 2003. The New Year was looking promising.

There may be people, true professionals, who carry into a meeting nothing but the agenda and their skills. For me, however, and perhaps for many others, it happens differently. I am emotionally primed wherever I go, ready to approve, reject, support, defend, even to go into all-out attack mode. A whole battery of emotions is permanently ready to fire. And I make no claim to consistency. If I am feeling mellow, things which at other times would bring rage to my heart will get past without a flicker.

I am also trailed wherever I go by a multitude of ghosts.

These ghosts follow me into every meeting, each one a hovering presence, ready to tweak or whisper into my ear at any time. They are a varied lot. The main one, who has haunted my life from the age of five, is I hope alive and well, probably a granny by now, although the face that peers over my shoulder is that of a little girl. Her name is Oonagh, and in my mind she will always be five. She is small, pale and thin, in a patched grey school uniform. We were at primary school together in Oban, a beautiful, sheltered ferry-and-fishing port in the west of Scotland. Like me, she used to hang around the edges of the riotous playground. We came, shyly, to like each other, and one day, shyly, I responded to her diffident invitation and went home with her after school. My family lived high on the equivalent of Nob Hill, in a beautiful three-storey house with some of the most spectacular views in Britain, looking west across the islands to the glory of Hebridean sunsets. It turned out that Oonagh lived with her large family in a crowded council flat, without a view. Their welcome of me as Oonagh's friend was unfussy in a friendly, busy way, but I was appalled by the crowding and the smells of damp and cooking. My family was rich, while this girl, whom I loved, was poor. I knew with all my soul that she did not deserve that. Much of what I have done in my life has been driven by my memory of Oonagh. She is always there with me, a reminder that the way things are is not the way they should be – that we can make them different, and that we should.

Many of the ghosts are good people. Mencius is there, the great Confucian philosopher for whom it was self-evident 2400 years ago that human nature is good – why else would we all leap instinctively to save a child teetering on the edge of a well? For him, the main purpose of a ruler was to care for his subjects. He gives me the confidence that in the right circumstances people will respond, and that power can be about doing decent things for people rather than about glory or wealth for the ruler.

Also hovering among the ghosts, invisible but ever present, is my late uncle, David Russell. As fifth-generation chairman of our extended family's 1200-employee paper mill, he wrote in a company document that his approach to management was based on a love for every single employee. It was true. He was born into great wealth in 1915, and brought up to hunt, shoot, fish and travel. My guess is that he was stimulating company for a number of girls from similarly privileged families: decades later I have seen the mention of his name smooth out wrinkles and put a gleam in the eyes of now respectable matrons. He fought all through the Second World War as an officer in the Black Watch infantry, beside the ordinary folk who would otherwise have been working in his paper mill. Along with his friends he often faced disciplinary procedures for bad behaviour when on leave. His parents thought he had fallen in with a bad lot, but his wife told me after he died that in fact it had been he who led *them* into trouble.

In the first attack at Alamein in North Africa, after three years of defeat for Britain, his unit was to storm during the night a key ridge rising above the flat desert and then hold it against the inevitable counter-attack by Rommel's highly competent army. He was wounded as the operation started, was patched up in a forward hospital tent, discharged himself to get back into the fight, worked all night to organise supplies going forward, and was then cut off for two days on the ridge under heavy bombardment. Wounded again, he was one of only two officers left alive when they were relieved. But they held the ridge. Alamein was Britain's first victory and David Russell was awarded the Military Cross.

He fought also in Sicily and Italy, and his war ended in 1944 when his leg was blown off in Normandy. In those years of fighting he came to love the ordinary folk fighting beside him. When your life is at risk you do not fight for ideals or for King and Country – you fight for those alongside you. It is on them that your life depends, as do their lives on you. After the war my uncle went back to his inherited role as their employer. He laid the foundations on which my first employee-buyout was built, not least by passing on his conviction that a leader must work in the interests of everyone he leads. When I took over from him as chairman of the paper mill, many family members wanted to sell their shares, and the only way to achieve that while sustaining a love for the employees was an employee-buyout. It worked like a dream, and I was hooked. He stays with me still, reminding me of the gentleness of heroes; of the fact that you do not have to use your power simply in your own self-interest; of the possibility of no-nonsense love for all people.

Among them too is what turned out to be a fantasy version of Chairman Mao. My life was irrevocably changed when I was twenty-four years old by his injunction to learn from the people before trying to lead them. Only much later did I find out about the millions who died because of his policies and his callousness; at the time he was still an inspiration. After my privileged upbringing, his phrase made me realise that I knew nothing of ordinary people, who, unlike me, had had to work from an early age. In some ways I thought they were lucky – at least they had been brought up by their parents rather than in unloving boarding schools. But Chairman Mao's *Little Red Book* helped me recognise that I knew nothing of them. So in 1972 I swapped my Oxford accent for an only intermittently convincing Scottish brogue, signed on as an unskilled labourer on a Taylor Woodrow building site beside Edgware Road tube station in London, and set out to learn from the workers. Soon I was elected shop steward and a national strike was organised by the union. The leaders wanted to limit the strike to just a few key sites, so that the rest of us, working on, could subsidise the strikers. As a believer in Mao, and along with many young shop stewards, I wanted to pull everyone out, to hit the employers hard. With my newly proletarian accent I ended up making inflammatory speeches to national gatherings of shop stewards. At one of these in Westminster Hall, in a state of excitement, having just made a speech to several hundred shop stewards, and hearing a rousing call to action from the other shop steward on my site, I forgot myself. When he made a particularly good point, I inadvertently reverted to my plummiest Oxford debating tones and called out at the top of my voice, 'Hear Hear!' Every delegate turned to look and I ran for the door.

I learned a lot during the strike: not only about ordinary working people, but also about the revolutionary left-wing groups, one of which I joined. I also learned about the press, whose campaigns against violence on the picket lines backfired, to my delight. They built up such a fear of violent flying pickets, mainly the product of their own fetid reactionary imaginations and cynical efforts to sell more papers, that they once helped me pull a large building site out on strike against the policy of the union, and all on my own. The managers let me speak to the workers, and the workers docilely stopped working, because they were all afraid of the violent flying pickets that according to the *Daily Mail* and the *Daily Express* would otherwise descend. Mao's instruction worked, and I learned from the workers. Above all I learned that working people are usually decent, trying to make a go of things. For me, the lasting lesson from Mao's idea is to listen to everyone, not just to the educated and the visibly successful. But I was cured of the dream of revolution by working as a teacher in China during 1974–6, Mao's last two years. I saw that under the so-called 'Dictatorship of the Proletariat' the reality was a nightmare, with political gangsters prospering while the ordinary people lived in fear.

Another ghost is Earl Sasser, professor of Production and Operations Management at Harvard Business School where, having been cured of revolution by working in China, I did my MBA. Earl Sasser filled our lives with energetic challenge, in a drawling voice from the deep south. He led us through case study after case study, often with sketched diagrams and lots of maths, showing what a difference it makes if operations are properly designed; how production is intimately integrated with all the other business functions (in analysing a case study he would require us to start by looking not at the operations but at the market and the employees); and how important it is to have leaders who understand the business rather than simply knowing finance. He also enabled me to see the extraordinary efforts people make when they cooperate because they are inspired, as opposed to manipulated or bullied. He showed us all that it is innovation that makes companies' performance take off, and that innovation in operations often comes from gaining voluntary, committed cooperation from *all* involved, not just the managers. His role is to remind me that it is not capital markets but committed innovation that builds real wealth. And it is people who innovate and commit themselves.

Also among the presences always with me is Isabella James, a woman in her fifties, a tough version of Oonagh. Isabella was elected in the late 1980s to the top council in the paper mill where I was chairman. She had won the support of her colleagues because she was suspicious of everything that managers did, and because she was prepared to stand up to them. We had started giving out shares, free, to all the employees, and she was elected to find where the catch was. At all the meetings for two years she sat hunched and glowering with her arms crossed, saying little. Then one day she understood that it was for real – we really were serious about giving out information to all the employees, and involving them in improving how things were done, and sharing the profits. And that we really were planning to buy all the family shares into a trust for the employees. She was transformed by this realisation. An unskilled worker, she became a great ambassador for employee-ownership, even travelling to the United States to address a huge conference on the subject. I don't imagine they understood much that she said in her strong Fife accent, but I am certain they understood the energy and passion that she communicated with every ounce of her strong body. Isabella was so used to her place at the back of the queue, neglected and manipulated by educated and powerful managers, that the possibility of being a genuine participant, encouraged and allowed to play a constructive role, was at first inconceivable to her. And when she saw that it was happening, it transformed her life. Her presence is there to remind me to keep at it, that no matter how many disappointments there are, no matter how long it takes for some people to catch on, the struggle remains absolutely worthwhile.

Philip Baxendale is the last of the good ghosts. As mentioned already, together with his cousin, Joan Caselton, he owned Baxi, the top manufacturer of domestic boilers in the UK. When he retired in 1983 he and his cousin transferred 90 per cent of the company's value to a trust for its employees: it was valued at £50m and they sold it to the trust for £5m. People like that appear once

in a century if we are lucky. It took time for everyone
working in the company to understand that it really was
theirs, but over the next sixteen years, latterly through
positive involvement of the employees, they made their
factory the most productive in the industry in Europe.
Then, in just fifteen months, a hubristic and self-serving
chief executive, together with a new big-name City chairman and what turned out to be a cynical fee-chasing
merchant bank, wrecked the company through engineering a huge acquisition, many times bigger than Baxi itself.
At the time of the acquisition in September 1999 Baxi
was valued at £150m; fifteen months later the operations
had to be sold for £26m. Poor strategic decision-making
had destroyed over £120m, five-sixths of all that had
been built up, and the employee-ownership was ended.

The fund that I now came to lead, the one that backed
the employee-buyout of Loch Fyne Oysters, consisted of
the £20m that was left in the trust after the debacle. Philip
Baxendale's presence on my shoulder keeps the vision
vibrantly alive and at the same time reminds me that it
has to be practical, that we have to be ready to deal with
people who are cynically greedy, and that principles must
be made to work in the real world if they are to count.
To do that, we have to be ready to push and cause trouble
when the situation demands it.

One of the main themes among the good ghosts is the
humane and unselfish use of power – not as an indulgence,
against the dictates of efficiency, but to unite and inspire
people to great things. That is what happens with
employee-ownership when it is done right.

Also hovering over my shoulder are evil spirits – Mao
has settled among them too, as I have learned more about

him. The theme of the evil ones is the abuse of power. They range from primary school teachers who beat me unjustly to powerful leaders who tortured and murdered their own people. Among them are the 'democratic' leaders who launched a war of aggression against Iraq in March 2003, just a couple of weeks before the Loch Fyne Oysters employee-buyout was completed: their lesson for me is that we have to keep control of our leaders, or else we are done for. This is as true in a company owned by its employees as in a country. Constitutional provisions for limiting the concentration of power are vital. But in the end it is up to individuals to make sure that these work, by supporting effective leaders while at the same time resisting the self-aggrandisement of the powerful. That takes courage.

One of the glories of employee-ownership is that the big cheeses report at the end of the year to the people they manage during the year. They also stand down periodically and offer themselves for re-election by these people. In this way power runs in a circle. It is a far better system than in a 'normal' company, where power runs down from the shareholders to the directors to the managers, with the employees, powerless in many ways, only ever given a voice to the minimal extent necessary to gain their cooperation.

12. 'Is This for Real?'

Trailing this cloud of mentors and ghosts, I arrived in pale winter sunshine at Loch Fyne Oysters. I sat in the car park for a moment contemplating the shimmering sea loch and the surrounding mountains and then, full of anticipation, went in. The restaurant entrance is unassuming, the interior mainly of simple wood. I told the smiling woman at the entrance that I was here for a meeting, found myself fetchingly outsmiled by her, and stood at the bar to wait for Andy Lane.

He appealed immediately to my good ghosts. Tall and slim, hair thinning and streaked with grey, he was dressed like a Breton fisherman in dark blue, with an old worn shirt under a sweater. Smiling gently, he could not have been more unassuming. Soon we were sitting at a table at the quiet end of the restaurant, by the west wall with its large windows looking down the loch. We were joined shortly by Iain McGlashan, the finance director, in more normal business dress – even, like me, wearing a tie.

Andy Lane began.

'I'd like to hear more about what Baxi Partnership does – sounds too good to be true.'

I explained about Philip Baxendale's massive generosity, about his feeling when he came to retire that he would not be able to face himself if he sold out the employees who had helped him build his boiler-manufacturing company, about how he had set up the trust which now, after many vagaries, was a fund which helped medium-sized companies exactly like Loch Fyne Oysters to pass into employee-ownership rather than being sold to big corporations.

Iain McGlashan and Andy Lane looked at each other.

'You do realise that we are not in a position to make a gift? The company has been up for sale for months. There will be offers from at least four bidders, we think. The shareholders will take the highest bid.'

I explained that the owners would be paid a fair market price. If it involved a gift from the sellers, there would be few employee-buyouts.

There was visible relief.

'OK, so how does it work?'

'It's simple really. We want the company to end up in the hands of the employees. But they can't afford to buy it – it might cost as much as £40,000 per person. So the company finances it. You – Loch Fyne Oysters – set up a trust for your employees. Then that trust borrows enough money to buy all the shares. In this way the trust comes to own the company, on behalf of all the employees. Simplicity itself.'

Iain McGlashan, looking sceptical, asked how the trust would repay the loan.

'The company guarantees the loan – so the lender knows that the cash will come from the profits of the company.'

'But the bank won't lend us enough money – it'll only lend us what it can get security over, maybe one and a half million. It'll probably take four million to buy the company.'

I explained that that was where Baxi Partnership came in. We would lend up to £2m of risk money. The bank would get priority and we would come behind the bank.

'So you buy shares?'

'No, the point is that all the shares are owned by the employees and by the trust for the employees. We just lend the money.'

Iain McGlashan, the accountant, the man whose job was to make sure that the finances were sound and that nothing was done unless it promised a decent financial return, was looking incredulous now.

'Why would you do that?'

Because we were owned by the trust set up by Philip Baxendale, I said. The purpose of the trust was to help strong companies become employee-owned. The whole point was to enable employees, led by professional managers, to buy the company where they worked. Obviously the fund had to make money to keep going, so the interest rate for this risk money would be higher than the bank's, but the purpose of the fund was not to make money. It was to help them get hold of their company.

Andy Lane, who had been watching, weighing it all up, came in again.

'Do I have to sell all my 40 per cent of the shares? I'd like to keep at least some of them.' This was the man who had devoted twenty-five years to building the company, who had shaped it and inspired the loyalty of so many around him. It was no surprise that he wanted to stay involved.

I explained that he did not have to sell everything. He could keep some shares – in fact everyone would find that reassuring, probably. Certainly we in Baxi Partnership would. Up to 25 per cent of the shares could stay with employees who owned them already. That would also help with the funding, because if they didn't sell them, those shares wouldn't have to be paid for. So if the company was worth £4m and existing shareholders held on to 25 per cent, they would only have to find £3m to complete the deal instead of £4m. Then they could sell the remaining 25 per cent gradually over the years to the trust.

In fact we would worry if an owner wanted to sell out completely – it would suggest that maybe he or she expected the performance to go down, and wanted to get out while the going was good. But if anyone held on to more than about 25 per cent, the employees would not feel that it really was their company.

'Trusts are run by trustees. You appoint the trustees, do you?'

'No, you do. The board of Loch Fyne Oysters will appoint half of the trustees, so that they can make sure that there are trustees capable of running the trust's practical affairs. The employees elect the other half. That way the trustees are always in touch with how people are feeling. Anyone can stand for the position of elected trustee.'

'Sounds pretty good to me so far,' said Andy Lane. 'Maybe we really will be able to do a John Lewis.'

Philip Baxendale's model had adopted a lot from John Lewis. The company would always be controlled by the trust, just as in John Lewis. The only difference was that the Loch Fyne employees would be given shares every year, with the result that over time each person would build up a personal stake. Whereas the John Lewis trust held all their shares for ever, the trust in Loch Fyne Oysters would hold at least 50 per cent for ever, with up to 50 per cent being distributed over time to the employees as individuals, then bought back when they wanted to sell. The aim was to give them a more direct connection with the company. John Lewis got a good connection by sharing the profits; we considered that, in addition to sharing the profits in cash, having shares added an extra dimension.

The eight long-serving managers who had been given options over shares would be able to exercise these options and buy the shares. Provided they held on to most of them, that would help with the funding too. We agreed that Andy Lane and the managers would retain a maximum of 25 per cent between them.

'So how do the other employees get their shares?' asked Iain McGlashan.

I was sketching on a sheet of paper. So far I had the Loch Fyne Oysters company, a circle, and the Loch Fyne Oysters trust, a box, linked by a line. I drew another box, representing another trust, a share incentive plan (SIP). I explained that each year, as long as the company was profitable, part of the profit would be passed to the SIP, which would use the money to buy shares and transfer them free into the direct personal ownership of each employee. That is how each person would have his or her own personal stake. They would also be able to buy shares if they wanted. The whole thing was highly tax-efficient – neither the company nor the employees would pay tax. The scheme was set up in 2000 by Gordon Brown, then Chancellor of the Exchequer, a long-term supporter of employee-share ownership.

There would therefore be two trusts, one to hold the main block of shares indefinitely and one to distribute some of the shares tax-efficiently to all the employees. Without a block of shares held collectively, the whole thing could become unstable, and without the individual shareholding it would be less immediate, less real, to each employee.

After we had talked it through for a couple of hours, Andy Lane took me round the operations. We visited everywhere, saw the simple offices and the slicing room, where we had to dress in special clothes to make sure it stayed clean, drove round to the oyster depuration plant – the tide was in so we did not see the oysters themselves – and went out on the loch in a battered fibreglass open boat, to see the mussels hanging in great clusters down heavy ropes under rows of black buoys.

Now that Loch Fyne Oysters was there, it seemed natural that it should be there. What could be more obvious than to farm oysters and mussels and have a fish restaurant at the head of the loch? At that time I had no inkling of what it had taken to put it there.

We agreed that Iain McGlashan would work on the financial projections and that I would meet up with Bob Craig, who had succeeded Johnny Noble as chairman. The aim would be, as soon as practicable, to set up the Loch Fyne Oysters Employee Trust and have it make a bid for the company.

As I drove home, it was impossible not to smile and whistle by turns. Loch Fyne Oysters would make a perfect employee-buyout.

13. The Deal

The first step was to meet with Bob Craig, the chairman. He was skiing in Courchevel, as he did for three weeks every January. By chance I was booked to go there too, for a week's skiing with my son.

An evening conversation fresh off the ski slopes feels different from a normal business meeting. You are well exercised, physically tired and relaxed, content at having survived the occasional testing moment at high speed, with or without a crunching fall or two. Over a couple of whiskies, I talked of my experience passing the family paper mill into employee-ownership, explained the history of Baxi Partnership and sketched out how an employee-buyout could be made to work in Loch Fyne Oysters. Bob Craig was easy to talk to, canny and to the point in his questions. He did not obviously warm to the idea, in the way that Andy Lane had, but nor was he against it: he was prepared to think it through in a rational way. His financial expertise shone through, and he was quick to understand the roles played by the trust and by Baxi Partnership's financing, something which is not always easy to grasp. This was clearly a man who would be good to have on your side in a business deal. Quick-thinking, on the ball, expert. Knowing that he was over seventy years old, I was impressed.

When the time came for me to ski back in the twilight

to join my son for our evening meal, we shook hands warmly. We would give it a try.

In a normal business acquisition there are two sides, and they are against each other. Even if there are mutual gains that can be made, in the end it comes down to a negotiation over a zero sum game: what one gains, the other loses, and vice versa. Each side employs corporate lawyers who are skilled at this game. They are often charming people, but they are adept at the little ploys that will wind up the other side, and ruthless at making the most of every possible advantage. An employee-buyout is quite different. Once the price is agreed, both the sellers and the buyers are working on the same side, to get everything designed to give the company the best chance of long-term success in employee-ownership. Making the switch from antagonism to cooperation is not always easy for a lawyer trained in the normal hostile process, but Patrick Stewart, the lawyer for Loch Fyne Oysters, got the idea quickly. Still, everyone involved had to pore over every paragraph repeatedly until there were no remaining differences and doubts. The main document was the Investment Agreement, and it was backed up by the Loan Agreement, new Articles of Association, a Trust Deed and a large number of less prominent but equally essential documents, few of them written in normal English, most in legalese. It seemed an endless task, but within a couple of months the paperwork was ready.

At the same time, Iain McGlashan was working almost obsessively on his computer, forecasting again and again different scenarios for the future performance of the business. He estimated that a price a little below £4m should be enough to win the battle with the other bidding companies. The first thing was to be sure that even if the performance of the company was poorer than expected, it could still bear the costs of the borrowings. The last thing anyone wanted was to load the company with a burden of debt that might drive it under. Better to be owned by another company than to go bust.

But what if the price was 25 per cent higher? Setting the price was outside anyone's control – it would depend on what the other companies bid. The predictions showed that Loch Fyne Oysters could pay for an employee-buyout at a price up to about £5m, though it would be tight. It could only succeed at that price if future performance improved continuously, without a blip. It would be risky to count on that.

So far the involvement of the employees had been minimal. Andy Lane had kept the managers informed, and they had been answering questions put by the employees, but there had been no organised communication. This would have to be addressed – it would be nonsensical to set up an all-employee buyout that the employees themselves didn't know was happening. Employees are used to having things done to them, rather than choosing to do things themselves, but the whole point of owning the company was that now things would be different: now they would be fully involved. In recognition of that, it was essential to give everyone the experience of participating in the decision – to make the decision theirs in reality. There would therefore be no buyout unless the great majority voted for it. Baxi Partnership never supported an employee-buyout unless that was the case. It was agreed that meetings would be held to explain to all the employees what was planned, to give them the opportunity to think about it, discuss it and vote on it.

At the same time, however, we had to wait until it looked likely that the buyout would go through, before telling everyone about it. If all the employees were told about it, and then the employee bid failed, they would feel that the acquirer had stolen their company from them. The winner would take over a company staffed by people who had had their hopes raised to an undreamt-of peak and then dashed – a perfect formula for resentment and hostility.

So the employee meetings were planned to take place immediately all the bids had come in, when it would be clear whether the employee bid would succeed. In the end the carefully provisional outside bids left plenty of room. The employee-bid team topped the best of them by putting in a clean bid, without caveats or qualifications, of just under £3.9m. They were in a position to win.

At the back of the site, unseen by the visitors to the shop and the restaurant, there was a collection of unattractive but serviceable modular huts. They were used as meeting rooms, a canteen and even offices. One grey day in March 2003 the employees filed out across the muddy yard to the biggest one. Bob Craig, Andy Lane and I spoke, explaining what was planned, and was now possible.

It is never easy for everyone to absorb a mass of new and complex information. For example, the idea of a trust is usually hazy at best for most people, but the roles of the trust, and of elected trustees, were key elements in the buyout. This meeting, nonetheless, was one of the most enjoyable of my working life. It is sheer delight to tell people, whose horizons have never included the possibility of anything but working as employees, that they and their colleagues look set to win control of their company and together become the owners. They will share by right in the wealth they all create, and their representatives will take part in all key decisions. With so much to take in, there was as always a fairly quiet response to the presentation, itself pared down to the key points only. Then came a whole series of questions, and for some, at least, a dawning understanding. They went away to think about it for a day or two, asking more questions as they occurred. Then a secret ballot was held: 100 per cent in favour.

All that remained now was to finalise and sign the legal documents.

The employees of Loch Fyne Oysters had chosen their future.

14. 'It's Ours!'

The day the buyout was completed, 4 April 2003, was just a normal spring day. The sky was grey, the clouds hanging low, hiding the tops of the mountains. A cold breeze danced its way up the valley, ruffling the dark sea loch and stirring the trees around the whitewashed buildings – the restaurant, the shop, the smokehouse and the slicing room.

However, there was one momentous difference for the people working there. On this ordinary day the buildings and the business became theirs. From then on they were no longer working for someone else, however much respected and admired; they were working for themselves, together.

The actual signing of all the documents to complete the deal was a lengthy process. Everyone gathered in the big main room at Ardkinglas House. This was where Johnny Noble had held his last meeting with Andy Lane and Bob Craig. The lawyers arranged the documents in order round the large dining-room table, and orchestrated the complex series of signings.

After all this had been completed, and celebrated with a cheerful glass of champagne for all involved, I walked into the shop at about lunchtime. The middle-aged women serving behind the counter were dressed as usual in blue shirts and yellow aprons, with clean white hats giving them an authentic fishwife appearance. They looked at me.

'Well?'

'It's yours!'

'Yesss!' said one. Another gave a little skip, incongruous at her age, which simply heightened the intensity of delight. Everyone was smiling. What a relief. No takeover by the men in suits, from a big corporation. And what a prospect. Their own company. They would make it successful; they would share the rewards.

A story like this deserved some publicity. It was only a small company, but the feel-good factor was huge. The implications too: if they could do it, anyone could. To make it even more attractive to newspaper editors, we decided to make a range of photographs available to the press. The photographer Ashley Coombes busied himself arranging shots of Andy Lane and others, and of employees, now employee-owners, serving one another in the restaurant, some posing as customers. Then he got a group of employees, dressed in their working uniforms and carrying a large tray overflowing with seafood, to row across the loch in the working boat from the mussel farm; up to his chest in the water, he took pictures of them standing precariously in the boat, all of them grinning, with the Oyster Bar in the background. This insanely unrealistic and superbly symbolic picture was used by a number of newspapers. Even the *Financial Times* reported the story with some prominence, and with a photo, though they used an archive picture of the wrong place. Johnny Noble would have been delighted and enraged at the same time, and would have sent an immediate letter of protest, filled with repetitions of the name 'Loch Fyne Oysters'.

Suddenly, after the signing and the photography were

over, no one knew what to do next. Perhaps Johnny Noble would have dreamed up some appropriate form of extended celebration, but even then there would have come a time to return to work.

Getting back to work was an anticlimax. I had made a point of saying to everyone that actually nothing much would change, but it was still a surprise for them. Everything was different, and yet nothing was different. They were still working at the same jobs, with the same people, led by the same managers. The same problems were there: the same panics meeting the same deadlines, the same people doing the shouting. The same pleasures were there too, of course: the satisfaction of doing a good job, of getting the next lorry dispatched on time, of seeing the last couple leave the restaurant in the evening, carrying the spirit of Loch Fyne in their smiles.

But when there has been a seismic shift, a revolution almost, people expect more. Surely since the company belonged to them now, things would change in some obvious way? There had to be some way in which it would actually make a difference. Expectations had soared.

In fact the switch to employee-ownership, while a fundamental change, is a change that stays in the background. It doesn't leap out and hit you every day. In any business the question of ownership is rarely at the forefront as people go about their daily tasks. At Loch Fyne Oysters they did think and talk about it, but it was not constantly in their minds. As usual they thought about what they had to do and how they were getting on with their workmates and their managers, not who owned the company.

Why didn't she speak to me, the toffee-nosed git?

He needs to pull his finger out if we're going to get that lorry off tonight.

That was a right laugh today, in the tea break.

And so on. Just the normal stuff of working life.

Gradually over time, however, people can begin to feel like owners. Attitudes can change as if by osmosis, responding to the background fact of ownership. Whether this process is fast or slow, deep or shallow, depends to a huge extent on the efforts of the managers. If they don't get to grips with the new ownership structure and its implications, hoping to sustain the comfortable (or even, strangely, the uncomfortable but familiar) old ways of doing things, the ride will be bumpy and the results uncertain. But if they work at understanding the changes and grasping the opportunities, they can activate the huge potential of shared ownership.

In any case, even with the best of goodwill and a genuine sustained effort to make it work, it tends to be years before the company's culture becomes an ownership-culture.

PART TWO

Making Employee-ownership Work

You can never have a revolution in
order to establish a democracy.
You must have a democracy in
order to have a revolution.

G.K. Chesterton
The Wind and the Trees

15. Constitutions

The extent of the changes that follow an all-employee buyout becomes clear only gradually to those involved; meanwhile the main focus must be to keep the business successful. There is little time for reflection and ways of doing things that have worked well in the past are deeply ingrained.

Up until now, the situation in Loch Fyne Oysters had been simple.

Who makes all the key decisions? The two founders.

Who do you have to go to if there is a significant problem? Either of the two founders.

Who do you have to tell if anything important happens? Either of the two founders.

Who decides which ideas are put into practice? The two founders.

Who gets all the profit? The two founders.

It wasn't difficult to understand, and all involved had developed a whole set of habits and expectations that reflected and sustained this basic structure.

Looking back some three years after the buyout, Virginia Sumsion, the marketing manager, put it like this:

> Johnny and Andy had set it up and were so used to making all the decisions and having to stand by them that they weren't used to letting other people have a say.

That was true even on the board, where the non-executives found it frustrating to have formal decisions ignored, or changed without discussion. It was equally clear on the shop floor and throughout the company, although because expectations were lower there was less frustration.

Anne Stewart, human resources manager:

It had been traditional, 'I say, you do.'

Marby Montgomerie, dispatch worker:

You were just always used to Andy and Johnny being the bosses. Everyone's just been so used to having Andy there, as the main man.

The result was a low level of involvement. David Mac-Donald, fish filleter:

Before the buyout it was just coming in and doing my job and going home and not really knowing what was going on. I didn't have a clue really. All I knew was that it was my job to fillet fish and go home.

There is of course no criticism implied here. Given the history, the long and often desperate struggle to establish the business, and the total commitment of the two founders, and given a world in which this is the dominant model for how a business should run, there is nothing to criticise.

But the change in ownership meant a change in the basic structure of these relationships, and of the relationships throughout the company. At first the old habits simply continued, and would have continued for ever, moving forward in a straight line like a satellite in space until a force was exerted to change the direction. The force came from the changed constitution of the company, designed in consultation with Baxi Partnership to reflect the threefold purpose: keeping the business successful, sustaining the employee-ownership, and involving everyone as partners. Broad lessons from the history of employee-owned companies, both in the UK and internationally, were incorporated into this constitution, but as always there would be room for improvement over time.

16. Business Leadership

Keeping the business successful was the overriding concern of everyone involved, as it had been before the buyout. There would be little point in spreading ownership and involving everyone if the business failed. This imperative was felt more widely than simply at board level. Greta Cameron:

> Like Andy, we wanted to make sure that this was going to work. You didn't want people to be able to say, 'Now that Johnny's dead the place is going downhill.' And it didn't. It was successful because the people were behind it.

David Attwood, operations director, expressed a similar feeling:

> For a lot of people employee-ownership has increased the pressures to succeed, not to make a mess of it.

One of the main lessons from experience elsewhere was the importance of leadership and leadership succession – finding good people to take on the senior roles when the time came. The quality of decision-making and of the implementation of decisions is perhaps the key factor in the success of any business, however the ownership is structured. When the company is owned by all its employees, there is an extra dimension. If the MD has a real understanding and feeling for the potential, it will tend to flourish; if he or she doesn't get it or empathise with it, the opportunity may be missed and the ownership undermined.

By now the original two-man board had expanded to include, in addition to the two non-executives, Simon Briggs the sales director, David Attwood the operations director, Iain McGlashan the finance director, and Allan MacDougall the production director. These individuals would bear the brunt of the task of keeping the business successful at the same time as leading the changes.

To help them, Baxi Partnership had the right to appoint one additional non-executive director. The aim was to find someone with relevant business experience, ideally someone who had worked in a company owned by its employees. The perfect person appeared in the form of Jane Burgess, who sat on the board of Waitrose, the food-retailing arm of the John Lewis Partnership. This made her the ideal candidate: someone with sound food-retailing experience in the foremost employee-owned company in the UK. As a strong individual with clear views she made an impact immediately. An effective non-executive director will often stir things up a bit, and at first the 'old guard' did not find it easy to accept her contributions, but over time she became a valued member of the board.

The normal reaction to the idea of employee-ownership is instinctively positive, some variation on the theme of:

> Of course you'll work harder and be happier if you have a stake in the company.

The instinct is right: you do work harder, and it is more satisfying. Everyone understands that; it seems self-evident as readily to an elderly housewife as to a young businessman, as natural for a child as for an experienced worker.

Why do things ever seem self-evident? Because they are working with the grain of human nature. Some responses just seem obvious, not because that is the way *they* are, but because that is the way *we* are. Examples readily spring to mind. Most people would be distressed at a partner's infidelity; to respond with equanimity would be strange. A mother will tend to be watchful over her new baby. A soldier will fight with more determination against a foreign invader in his own country than if he is sent to occupy someone else's. These responses are deeply natural; they go with the grain of human nature. In the same way positive feelings develop in those who share the ownership of the company where they work.

When employee-ownership is discussed, however, there is often a flicker after the initial instinctive recognition, a 'too good to be true' second thought. For many people life is disappointing. They have seen hopes dashed and trust betrayed. They are used to being taken advantage of by people with more education or experience, used to losing out to people with better connections or luck or just quicker wits. This secondary response goes something like:

But will it really work? Won't the workers mess it up?

This is not instinctive in the same way as the positive initial reaction. It is the shadow cast by reason, sometimes amplified by fear and by ideas still prevalent about the place of workers and the impossibility of ordinary people getting things right.

One of the fears is that chaos will ensue, that there will be votes on all decisions, that the marketing policy will be decided democratically by the ignorant, and even expert managers will lose their authority. These fears were realised in the cooperatives set up by Tony Wedgwood Benn in the 1970s, attempting to rescue the Triumph motorcycle company among others. They failed, and even if the underlying businesses had been competitive they would probably still have failed, because business decision-making requires expertise – you need to have good, experienced leaders making informed decisions. For this reason the model implemented at Loch Fyne Oysters sustained the existing board and management structure. There *was* a difference – the transfer of ownership changed the ultimate reporting relationship – but that was not visible for some time. Meanwhile, it was business as usual.

Some of these doubts have been developed by economists into full-scale theories. There is the 'free-rider' theory: if people own the company together, it will fail because there will be too many free riders – people who do not pull their weight, but rest content to profit from the work of others. And there is the theory that the firm will be decapitalised – when they own the company the workers will tend to bleed it dry, taking a short-term, bird-in-the-hand approach, extracting cash rather than investing to keep the company strong.

These dogmas survive in the face of ever-growing empirical evidence to the contrary. Actually, there are large employee-owned businesses that have prospered mightily for decades, outperforming their conventionally owned rivals. At the time of writing there are numerous examples in the UK alone. It is worth looking briefly at a few of them.[10]

The John Lewis Partnership, mentioned earlier as having inspired Andy Lane to investigate employee-ownership in the first place, is the most consistently successful UK retailer. Now with over 60,000 'partners', John Lewis has for more than fifty years been wholly owned by a trust for all of them.

The globally successful engineering consultancy Arup, employing over 7000 people, designers of such structures as the Sydney Opera House and the bridge between Denmark and Sweden, has likewise been owned by employee trusts for over four decades.

PA Consulting Group, another internationally successful company, has been owned for a similar length of time by a combination of trusts for its 3000 employees and by the employees directly.

There are many more large companies controlled by their employees. There are also small employee-owned companies that have prospered, some against huge odds, surviving periods of competitive pressure that would have finished off businesses owned by outsiders. UBH, a subsidiary of a large corporation, was bankrupted in 1999 by the corruption and incompetence of some of its managers. Ninety-one newly redundant employees put up £5000 each to buy the assets of their company, which makes tanks to carry liquids in containerized transportation systems. Once the employees had bought the assets, they appointed an MD with experience in the industry, licensed the basic technology to a Chinese company, earned millions in royalties over the next few years, and used the cash to turn themselves into one of the leading manufacturers of cryogenic tanks in the world – a sophisticated technological achievement. At the ultra-cold temperatures at which cryogenic tanks operate, air turns to liquid, and if a rubber ball were dropped it would shatter rather than bounce.

Another example is Woollard and Henry, bought in 2002 by its twenty-five engineer-employees. The market for their product – 'dandy rolls', the cylinders that put watermarks into paper – then collapsed, but the commitment and creativity of the employee-owners enabled them to break into new markets, hugely increasing export sales, pulling the company through to prosperity and forcing the closure of their main competitor. Dynamism goes together with employee-ownership at least as naturally as it does with outside ownership, and more thoroughly, since all the employees are positively involved.

It is therefore not surprising that Scott Bader, one of the few independent specialist chemical manufacturers in an industry dominated by giants, has prospered for over fifty years in the ownership of a trust for its now 600 employees, expanding overseas and developing an outstanding reputation for innovation.

The closure of Tower Colliery was announced in 1994. Under local union leadership and against government and senior union opposition, the 239 miners each invested £8,000 redundancy money to buy the mine. Over the next thirteen years they mined it successfully and profitably. When the seam ran out in 2008 the closure was more like a festival than a wake.

The list could go on: the UK Employee Ownership Association in London has an ever-growing number of member companies – over fifty at the time of writing – ranging from the huge to the tiny. Each one is owned wholly or substantially by its employees, and together their turnover is over £20 billion.

Far from squeezing their companies dry as predicted by some economists, people in employee-owned companies tend to invest readily, to make sure the business stays strong. Usually they take out cash only when they are sure that it can be spared. In this they stand in marked contrast to many investors on the stock exchange, whose interest in companies is purely financial. Many outside investors will not hesitate to do things that damage the business in the longer term if by doing so they can get more cash out in the short term. Chief executives are often changed when the dividend falls. Mergers are frequently pushed through for the personal benefit of individuals involved, in spite of damage to the businesses. There is clear evidence that most takeovers destroy value; but they continue to be done, partly because top managers and advisers can profit personally from doing them.[11]

By contrast, when people together own the company in which they work, the vast majority not only work hard but do so with even greater commitment. Idlers gain an unenviable reputation – gossip is not kind in an employee-owned company when people are not pulling their weight. But mainly it is not the threat of muttering that keeps people working, but the fact that they identify with their company and want to do a good job.

There is more to human nature than is dreamt of in economics, which has been slow to recognise the role of social phenomena such as shared commitment. In classical economic theory, to be human is to be crudely self-interested in the short term. One economist, Robert Frank, has pointed out that an economist's worst nightmare is to be exposed in front of his or her peers as lacking in cynicism about human nature.[12] This one-dimensional view of people makes it easier to model their behaviour, at the cost of pushing the models further and further from reality. It makes the models utterly invalid when it comes to employee-ownership. If you build into your theory an assumption of purely self-interested individuals, then of course you will end up with prescriptions that are limited to purely self-interested behaviour. But you will fail to predict, or even to observe, the potential of shared commitment. It is as if a football commentator could see the goals but not the passes that led to them.

Provided that the leadership remained good and that the leaders were given the space to operate, there was good reason for confidence that everyone, working together, would be able to keep Loch Fyne Oysters successful.

At the time of the buyout in 2003, the message that was given out was not one of change. Following Johnny Noble's death the appointment as chairman of Bob Craig, already a familiar face on the board, and following the buyout the continuation of Andy Lane in the role of MD, both signalled a 'business as usual' approach. It seemed the least amount of disruption possible in the circumstances. That was reassuring, and it was backed up by a conscious effort to convey continuity. Virginia Sumsion, looking back later, felt that this might have been overdone, but was unavoidable.

We gave out the message that the buyout was happening and nothing was going to change. The directors were afraid that people would worry, so the message at the time was that nothing was going to change, which actually, looking back on it, I think was wrong. But none of us knew enough about it to explain what the changes were going to be, because it is only once it happens that you realise what it means. So I think there was a lot of trust in Bob and Andy to get it right.

In the senior management, however, change was soon brewing. Having given Loch Fyne Oysters so much for so long, Andy Lane began to feel that he wanted to step back. His long-term dream was beckoning ever more strongly: to spend time with his family, which was no longer virtual but real – by now he and his wife Liz had two small sons. In any case, it didn't seem right to cling on to the MD role, now that he had sold most of his shares to the employee-buyout. And having sold most of his shares, he could also afford to relax and spend time sharing in his sons' boyhood years.

The others on the board recognised that one of the benefits of Andy Lane stepping back would be to create more space for the directors and managers to operate. Given the deeply ingrained habit of referring everything to the founders, his continued presence might even turn into an obstacle. That fitted very well with his desire to spend more time with his family, and so a year after the buyout he moved to Cornwall, from then on returning to base at Loch Fyne only every third week or so. This had the added advantage for the business that he was able to investigate the fishing industry in the south-west, to find good sources of white fish, caught using sustainable methods such as line-fishing, much needed for their expanding sales. As the expert and the inspiration behind the commitment to sustainable fishing, he was the ideal man to do that, and his absence would allow the managers and new directors to flourish.

The move had mixed success. Andy Lane's family loved Cornwall, and he did find sources of white fish, as a result strengthening Loch Fyne Oysters' capacity to supply white fish in line with their ecological principles. And in his absence the managers did indeed begin to find their feet as decision-makers. It was when he was at base every third week or so that difficulties occurred. The habit worked both ways: the managers were used to referring things to him and he was used to making all the decisions. When he was away the managers would begin to make decisions, but when he was back he would express his views, sometimes all too clearly, that they were not making necessary changes fast enough. He was not only the inspiration behind the commitment to sustainable fishing; he was also the person who had chosen to lead the company into employee-ownership. He understood instinctively the change in management style that would be required to allow all the employees to become more involved and committed, and he sometimes felt that the managers were not moving quickly enough to develop that approach.

Relationships on occasion became strained – it was hard on them all. An entrepreneur who has built a company will always see it as a whole, and as something that can be changed and developed. For a manager working in a part of the business, that overall perspective and that confidence to make significant changes are harder to achieve – the business seems more of a given, more fixed. Andy Lane:

> I was trying to be Mahatma Gandhi, but succeeded only in being Joe Stalin. I was impatient to see fundamental change in the way we involved staff, and was too swift to condemn anything I felt fell too far short of the ideal. It was a difficult decision, but it really was time for me to go.

He reached this decision in spring 2005, after a full year of trying to make the new system work. Loch Fyne Oysters needed to find a successor for him. After defining the role and the characteristics of the perfect person, they began the search by talking to people in the trade. Jane Burgess, the non-executive director from Waitrose, had extensive experience in recruiting senior people, and made an important contribution.

The best candidate turned out to have been referred by Mark Derry, the MD of the restaurants. His name was Bruce Davidson, a Scot returning from the Far East with great depth of experience in achieving international growth in consumer brands, both tobacco and retail. Over several extensive interviews held during autumn 2005 and early 2006, he proved increasingly convincing and the appointment was made. Andy Lane, the wise old guardian of the vision, stepped back into a purely non-executive role, remaining active in searching out opportunities for good sources of fish, and helping in a large project to develop a distribution hub for customers in the south.

On the shop floor the view was pithily expressed to

Andy Lane that the tobacco industry was not an appropriate background for an MD of Loch Fyne Oysters. But
why should the bad guys get to keep all the expertise?
Andy Lane:

> We believed that nobody is irredeemable, and here was
> an apparent convert on the road to Damascus. Who were
> we to condemn?

From Bruce Davidson's point of view, the contrast
added to his motivation:

> I have moved from politically incorrect to politically
> correct in Loch Fyne. It's nice to be talking about a
> growing business, a growing sector, a sector that has got
> all positive rather than negative PR elements attached to
> it. It's quite a compelling mix – a great brand in the right
> categories. And the Scottish connection is important too.

Coming from an industry where brands were illusions
created around trends in public perceptions, he was
enthralled by the reality of what he was dealing with.

> The brand is real. It's been nurtured and developed and
> built over a sustained period of time. It's not reinventing
> itself to try to match what the consumer trend is – it's
> there, and it's been there, and it's been saying the same
> thing even when it wasn't fashionable to do so.

After holding senior positions in huge international
companies, leading Loch Fyne Oyster's 110 or so employees was a change for Bruce Davidson but he saw that

the potential of the business went far beyond the banks of the loch.

> One of the challenges I have is to make people see what a fantastic brand and fantastic business it is that they are part of. Even though it's a small business in a small part of Scotland, the potential for it to become a big international business is enormous. The goodwill that the brand has, in many parts of the country and many parts of the world, is really remarkable.

As expected, Bruce Davidson's approach to management was rather different from the entrepreneurial engagement of the founders. He sought to push decision-making out to the managers rather than centralising it, and started to develop people at every level more systematically than previously. As a result, some people soon began to show abilities that amazed those around them.

One of many effective ways of generating understanding and enthusiasm was to send small groups to the guinea-pig 'soft-opening' events of the new Loch Fyne Restaurants, now opening in quick succession all over England.

> You're filleting fish, 6000 fish a week or whatever it is, and you're packing it away and it's pouring with rain and it's miserable. So whether it's St Albans or Midhurst or Knutsford or Leeds or York or Gosforth, all of which we sent people to, they see the restaurants packed, they see the staff absolutely thrilled to be working for Loch Fyne Restaurants, they see the fantastic design of the restaurants, they see all the views of Loch Fyne and

sometimes even their own faces on the wall. All of that has a massive impact in getting them to see that this bit of fish that they're having to carve up and pack in a box eventually becomes a fantastic meal for somebody in a Loch Fyne Restaurant.

This approach fitted well with employee-ownership.

Even if you were just an employee you would feel proud, but you feel extra-proud when you can say, 'It's my company that's doing that.'

Bruce Davidson's presence and style encouraged the others, though they found it challenging to have to take full responsibility for decisions and for making sure that they were implemented.

He was initially disappointed to find that the anticipated ownership effect seemed muted. One Saturday shortly after his arrival, at the annual Food Fair held in large marquees next to the Loch Fyne Oysters site, he was dressed as a fishmonger, enthusiastically opening oysters for the crowds of visitors, an occasional famous actor among them. He remarked on the fact that fewer employees than he had expected had volunteered to help. Later he summarised his observation.

You don't get the marked 'I'm going to go the extra mile for the company' that I probably naively anticipated you would get. And you still get a lot of infighting. Again naively, we're all in this together, it's our company, so why can't we work better together?

However, the glass is undoubtedly half full. Christine MacCallum, the shop manager, smiles and is energised as she remembers a recent event.

> Years ago the staff didn't have a say, now they are listened to, and you can see they're so keen – the boys on the filleting and the girls in the office, keen to get on. We went up to Aviemore to a show recently. Linda asked me to help fill a counter there, for a tasting. I felt so proud of Loch Fyne Oysters and she did too – she was just beaming. We made a great job of it – we want to do a good job and really put Loch Fyne Oysters on the map.

It is clear from the history of employee-ownership in many companies that this 'going the extra mile' attitude takes time to percolate through the whole company, and it takes good, consistent, determined leadership. It is not only the employees who have to change, to commit themselves to the whole; it is also the leaders, who in a sustained way must show that they mean it, that this really is for everyone, that they can be trusted, that there is no reversion to using their power to look out for themselves, or simply because they can.

This is not exactly new – it is a recognition of how people have always responded. The philosopher Mencius, a sort of special adviser to a warlord in fourth-century BC China, saw it too.

'You should value the people most, yourself as leader least. In this way, winning the favour of the ordinary people, you will become Managing Director.' (He actually said 'Emperor' – modern company titles are different from those of war-torn states 2400 years ago. Yet people are essentially the same.)

In many businesses, this approach to leadership still seems pretty novel.

17. Owning the Company: Shares for Everyone

Acquiring the ownership of a company is expensive.

As mentioned before, Andy Lane had discussed the possibility of an employee-buyout with Johnny Noble, who had worried about the price they might have to accept, and also about saddling the employees with personal debt. The employees could never have afforded to buy the company themselves – in the end the buyout price equated to £32,400 per head, more than two years' earnings on average. Very few employees of a relatively low-paying company ever manage to save that sort of sum, and few would be able to borrow it.

The solution was to use a trust to buy the shares, with the finance guaranteed by the company. Since it was a trust whose only purpose was to benefit the employees, the employees indirectly owned the shares from day one, through trustees whose sole responsibility was to work in the employees' interests. And then, rather than having to pay off the debt personally, they would pay it off by making the company successful. Their personal wealth was not at risk, and they had the greatest possible incentive to make the company successful.

David Attwood, the operations director, had briefly considered trying to arrange a buyout by the managers themselves, but had soon given up because they just couldn't have raised enough capital. With that experience, he was impressed by the way that the employee-buyout was financed by the company itself, not by the individual employees.

> The buyout really surprised me. None of us had that sort of equity to put up for the company. It was a very elegant solution.

This form of leveraged buyout meant that the company itself carried a great deal of debt. Loch Fyne Oysters borrowed £1.5m from the bank, and a further £2m from Baxi Partnership. The bank's money was secured against the assets of the company, but there was no security left for Baxi Partnership, with the result that their money was at risk. The bank insisted that Loch Fyne Oysters would repay the bank's money first, and only then start repaying Baxi Partnership. So Baxi Partnership's money was not expected to be fully repaid for about ten years, and to create some leeway the agreement gave Loch Fyne Oysters up to fifteen years to complete the repayments. In return, in addition to normal interest payments, Loch Fyne Oysters agreed to make a payment to Baxi Partnership each year, related to the success of the company – in financial terms, an added-value-related risk-premium. The use of debt in this way achieved the goal of keeping all the shares in the hands of employees and the employee trust.

In America, the first person to use a leveraged buyout and an all-employee trust was Louis Kelso, who invented it in California in 1956 to enable the employees of Peninsula Newspapers to buy the company from its founders. In the UK John Spedan Lewis had done the same a few years earlier: in 1951 he passed his company into a trust for the employees in exchange for an interest-free loan of £1m, which he was paid over a period of some years. The two inventions were no doubt independent – Louis Kelso is unlikely to have heard of the John Lewis deal.

The two buyouts – Peninsula Newpapers and John Lewis – differ, however, in one significant characteristic: how long the companies subsequently remain employee-owned. Peninsula stayed in employee-ownership for twenty-two years, a respectable length of time, but that is dwarfed by the longevity of the employee-ownership of John Lewis, which celebrated its fifty years in 2001 and seemed set to continue indefinitely. Both companies are comfortably exceeded by La Ceramica, the most venerable employee-owned company in Italy, converted from conventional ownership in 1874. The time in Peninsula was limited in part by the type of trust used, which had to pass out all the shares eventually to the employees. As with many employee-buyouts where the shares were all held by the employees individually, it proved impossible to sustain a liquid internal market for the shares, and as a result the company was eventually sold.

Loch Fyne Oysters adopted an ownership structure designed to be stable for the long term. The simplest long-term structure is the one used by La Ceramica, John Lewis, Arup and Scott Bader. *All* the shares in these companies are held permanently in collective holdings, none of them by any individual. In the case of the British companies, this holding is in one or more trusts. Since, unlike a person, a trust does not die or need to buy a house or pay for a holiday, or put its kids through university, or show off its wealth to its peers, or suffer or enjoy any of the other ambitions and responsibilities of normal human beings, it never has to sell the shares. The main benefit it provides for its beneficiaries, the employees, is the happiness of experiencing the benefits of ownership – information, profit and power – without themselves directly owning the shares. The constitution of John Lewis puts it almost exactly in those words. The first principle in the constitution states:

> The Partnership's ultimate purpose is the happiness of all its members, through their worthwhile and satisfying employment in a successful business. Because the Partnership is owned in trust for its members, they share the responsibilities of ownership as well as its rewards – profit, knowledge and power.

The aim is thus to integrate, through a good constitution properly implemented, the various aspects of running a company. Owning shares is much more than having a piece of property that is valuable in monetary terms. You miss several tricks if you don't experience *all* the benefits of ownership – the knowledge, the involvement, the sharing in profit, and the power that belongs to all the shareholders acting together, the power to determine who are the leaders, and to shape what they do through engagement with them.

If a normal company – that is, the managers with the support of the shareholders – gives the employees a few shares each, that does not create this experience. No power rests in the hands of employees, who together own only a small fraction of the shares. They cannot influence the appointment of the leaders, or prevent the company from being sold and the new owners from acting in a rapacious way. Amazingly, however, there is powerful empirical evidence that even this kind of employee shareholding is associated with strong rises in productivity.[13] People are hungry to be part of something, and even crumbs make a difference. They want to do a good job, and are ready to respond positively if the barriers even look like being removed, the barriers created by those in authority when they treat people as assets to be exploited and order them about rather than engage them as partners.

So, incorporating lessons from the example of John Lewis and the other long-lived UK companies wholly owned by permanent trusts, the ownership of Loch Fyne Oysters was designed to keep 50 per cent of the shares permanently in trust for the employees.

The trust holding was not 100 per cent, because Philip Baxendale's vision in setting up the Baxi Partnership fund included a provision for individual ownership. He considered that owning some shares directly would give both the people and the business additional benefits. It would give each employee a direct, personal stake in the company. This he believed would have a greater impact on each person than having all the shares owned indirectly in trust. Each person would have a share certificate, an unmistakable statement of membership. He also felt that it was important to allow people to share in the value created by reinvesting some or all of each year's profit. If you own shares personally, any profit reinvested will tend to add to the value of your shares; if you hold no shares personally, you might be tempted to distribute the profits rather than reinvest them, which would undermine the business in the longer term. Actually, the highly successful companies mentioned have had a high rate of reinvestment; Philip Baxendale's aim was to try for an improvement beyond what was already a very effective system. The other 50 per cent of the shares in Loch Fyne Oysters were therefore made available for ownership by the employees individually.

A trust is not strictly a body, like a company: it is actually a legal relationship. The trustees hold the shares themselves, as individuals, but they do not hold them *for* themselves: they have a duty, backed up by a considerable body of law, to exert their powers as owners only in the interests of their beneficiaries, in this case the employees. They have been trusted by the person or company which set up the trust, the settlor, to look after the property and to use it in line with the original purpose and rules, which are defined in the trust deed. They are holding the shares in a relationship of trust with the original settlor and the beneficiaries.

Not everyone can rise to the occasion of being a trustee, setting aside personal interests, getting to grips with the purpose and the rules, and then using the property for the beneficiaries in the ways defined in the trust deed. Baxi Partnership had suggested that the trustees should be appointed in two ways: half by the board, who it was assumed would appoint people with appropriate expertise, and half through an election by the employees. Then the appointed and elected trustees between them could, if they felt the need, appoint a professional – a lawyer or accountant. An early decision by the directors, however, was that it would be best if the trustees were all elected. They also appointed a professional, Patrick Stewart, the company's lawyer, to keep them right, especially on statutory duties and procedures and other technical issues.

The next question was how to get shares into the hands of the employees. One of the principles agreed at the beginning with Baxi Partnership was that *every* employee should hold shares. It would not be sufficient if some people were employee-shareholders and others were simply employees: that would create a two-tier system, which would undermine the important feeling that 'This is *our* company.' It followed that at least some shares had to be given out free – if the shares were simply put up for sale, some people would not buy any, especially in a company like Loch Fyne Oysters with many fairly low-paid jobs. So to make sure that the shareholding was inclusive, a proportion of the profit would be used each year to distribute shares free. Anyone who had worked there for at least a year would qualify to receive shares.

There was an important unseen benefit to this decision to give out free shares. As mentioned before, many of the companies that have failed to sustain their employee-ownership, like Peninsula Newspapers, have done so because there were not enough employees buying shares to allow all who wanted to sell shares to do so. So in the end they had to allow employees to sell to outsiders, either by selling the company or by floating the shares on the stock exchange. But in Loch Fyne Oysters, since in every profitable year shares will be needed to distribute to the employees, those shares will have to be purchased. That means that there will be a significant buyer in the market in every profitable year. The share market will therefore be liquid – people are likely to be able to sell when they want to.

The first shares were distributed a few months after the buyout. The board and trustees together had decided to distribute them not as a percentage of salary but in proportion to length of service, to recognise the long years of work that had helped build the company. From the second year, they changed to equal distribution per head.

The initial reception of the shares was less than wholly enthusiastic. This is normal. When has anyone ever given you anything free, without a catch? Frances Bremner was working in the shop.

> When the shares came out people were maybe a bit sceptical. I remember some saying, 'It's just a piece of paper!' and 'What does it mean?' But that was at the beginning, and people know now.

Marby Montgomerie, in dispatch, was perhaps at the sceptical end of the scale, still muted in her views on shares some three years after the buyout.

> Well, it's something you never had.

But she was already thinking as a shareholder. She criticised some employees for being too demanding.

> They're all harping on – they want this and they want that – but that's just taking the company money away, and our shares will get less valuable.

The people working in the Oyster Bar with Greta Cameron were quick to understand shares, being forced to talk about it by customers intrigued by the wooden sign at the entrance, carved with the slogan 'Loch Fyne Oysters: a company owned and run by its employees'.

> That's what really brought it home to the staff, and often not just customers but suppliers too. They'll ask about it, and how it's going, when they phone in. A lot of people are inquisitive about the shares. You'll hear the staff saying to them, 'Yes we've got shares, we all own shares, and we're partners in it.'

In production, the learning was slower, but according to Raymond McCaffer, speaking some four years after the buyout:

> They're seeing it starting to pay off, with a nest-egg building up. They're seeing real benefits. They all seem to like the idea that they're part-owners of the company.

In the shop, Frances Bremner observed a similar effect.

> They look forward to getting their free shares. A couple of people sold shares last year and people hear about it and realise they've actually got something meaningful.

Raymond McCaffer observed in production a generally improved focus on the job, which he put down in part to this sense of ownership. Greta Cameron saw a particular effect in the Oyster Bar.

> It's helped in the Oyster Bar because if somebody has not been doing their job the others will say to them, 'Come

on – this is mine as well!' Or if somebody's misusing something they'll say, 'That's ours. It's not yours, it's ours!' So it makes them aware of what they've got and I think it's been very, very good.

In addition to receiving free shares, employees were invited to buy shares, again as part of the highly tax-efficient SIP. Most people felt that shares which they had bought would mean even more to them than shares which had been received free. Those who bought shares did so effectively at much less than half price, both because of the tax benefits and because the company offered matching shares.

Early on, Bob Craig felt quite inspired by seeing the wealth-spreading financial effect of share-ownership in practice.

I found it a tremendous thrill to go down to Strachur, as I did the other day, to make a retirement presentation to someone who had been with us for fifteen or twenty years. I handed her a cheque for £3500 or £4000. She hadn't realised it was coming, hadn't realised her shares would be sold and she'd get the money. Apart from a dog that savaged me at the door, everyone welcomed me with open arms when they discovered what this was about. It gives me tremendous pleasure to think that somebody can get the benefit of all those years of work.

The company had introduced a pension scheme in the early 1980s, as soon as it was stable enough to do so. Now, in addition to her pension, this employee received this quite magical-seeming lump sum, in cash, tax-free. This and similar events fed back into the body politic, turning heads and building confidence, gradually silencing the doubters.

Cash was very tight after the buyout, mainly because of the need to clear the bank debt and begin to pay back the loan from Baxi Partnership. While things did not go as well as the more optimistic projections, the company continued to thrive and in 2006, with some fanfare, declared a dividend, to be paid shortly before Christmas. At around the same time people could sell their shares for the first time, and there was some concern that many might sell, even though the payments would not be tax-free until the shares had been held for another two years. It would be tempting for low-paid people to gain windfall payments measured in thousands of pounds. The board needn't have worried. With tax to pay on sale and the dividend to gain by holding on, only two people sold.

Thus already Loch Fyne Oysters was spreading widely the wealth it was creating. In the first four years after the buyout, shares worth a total of £466,000 were distributed; in addition employees bought over £86,000 worth, and received the same again in matching shares. None of this cost the company any cash immediately. In the last two of these years dividends of nearly £100,000 were also paid. After a few years these shares could be sold. Once in the hands of those who sold the shares, a proportion of the money would feed into the businesses in the local community. The knock-on effects would multiply. Almost alone among communities in the developed world, Loch Fyne Oysters was reversing the trend towards the concentration of wealth – a reversal that many politicians yearn in vain to achieve. While only the cash dividend could be spent immediately, the rest would in time be sold, and likewise feed into the local economy. If the company did well meanwhile, of course, then the sums would be greater. These figures, spread among a little over 100 people, were already significant, and as the borrowings began to be repaid, and would be repaid in full in future, so more cash would be available to grow the company even faster, and to distribute among the employee-owners.

Moreover, Loch Fyne Oysters was doing this at the same time as becoming *more* productive as a business. In the year before the buyout, the average sales per employee was £66,000; in the following three years it grew by 40 per cent to over £92,000, a compound growth rate of nearly 12 per cent per annum. In the year to June 2007 the sales per head levelled out, as thirteen new people were recruited to bring the total to 124 employed, partly to build capacity for the next step up in growth. At the same time they were revamping their distribution system for the whole of the UK, and introducing a range of new ready-made meals. Jointly with the restaurants they owned the rights to the use of the names 'Loch Fyne Oysters' and 'Loch Fyne Restaurants' – now they were together licensing the first new restaurant abroad, in Dubai. Dynamism and growth were evident in every part of the company.

Growth and fairness: what an attractive combination. No wonder Bob Craig beamed as he handed over that cheque. This was a good thing, no doubt about it.

The contrast with a more common form of buyout, the management buyout or MBO, is clear. In an MBO the financial structure is also highly leveraged, and if the company is successful the value of the shares can rise, sometimes dramatically. But the shares are usually concentrated in the hands of the top few managers and their backers, the venture capitalists or 'private equity' investors. If the company is successful this brings great wealth to a few, often by reducing the proportion that is going to the less well-off employees of the company. In human terms, in social terms, in political terms there is no comparison. An all-employee buyout, where the employee-ownership is sustained, has a far more beneficial effect on the lives of its members and on the whole community around it.

An example of a successful MBO-and-private-equity deal is provided by Loch Fyne Restaurants itself. In 2005, well within the ten years from the initial investment that they had set as the target in 1998, Loch Fyne Restaurants, now Loch Fyne Oysters' biggest customer, organised for their shareholders to be able to sell and a private equity company to take a majority stake. David Sumsion's and Andy Lane's shares were sold for a small fortune – they had cost £1 per share in the initial investment and were now sold at £10 per share. The friends Johnny Noble had persuaded to invest in what at the time had been a risky new venture were paid out so handsomely that it was voted the best deal of the year by financiers in the City of London.

Mark Derry again:

It worked really well and was great fun and my only regret is that Johnny didn't see the transaction come to fruition. That's what he did it for: he wanted slates on the roof of Ardkinglas House. He achieved it, but without knowing it.

He pauses, then raises a quizzical eyebrow.

Maybe.

The restaurants were started with £1.2m and the model of the Oyster Bar at Loch Fyne. Eight years later the company's shares were worth £30m. A further two years after that, in August 2007, the chain had grown to thirty-six restaurants and was sold to the brewers Greene King for £68m.

By all the criteria of normal business, this is a tremendous success story. The idea was developed through tenacious entrepreneurial struggle into a viable business; it was expanded by bringing in managerial expertise and capital, and then the expansion was repeated with new capital again. Surely everyone benefited: the entrepreneurs and the expert managers and the people who risked their capital were all rewarded by making a fortune?

Yes. But there was one key player who gained little or nothing: Greta Cameron. Her case can represent the position of a typical employee.

Andy Lane recognises the part she played.

I doubt whether Loch Fyne Oysters itself would have
survived without the Oyster Bar under Greta's leadership
in the early days.

And without the Oyster Bar there would have been no Loch Fyne Restaurants.

But Greta Cameron was not an owner. When Johnny Noble and Andy Lane passed the two restaurants at

Nottingham and Elton into the new company, this was of course entirely proper. These two owned the company, which owned the restaurants. They were free to take out the restaurants and put them into another company if they wished.

The fact that Greta Cameron had worked so hard and effectively to make them successful was not relevant, because she was an employee, not a shareholder. Enormous value was eventually created by turning these two restaurants into a chain. Her contribution had been crucial. But this value belonged wholly to the two founders and to the wealthy people who put in their cash, and not at all to Greta Cameron. The founders had worked tirelessly and brilliantly to make the original business succeed; but Greta Cameron and other employees had also worked tirelessly and creatively and enthusiastically, far beyond the call of duty, also to make everything succeed. Then, when the value was cashed in, the founders and investors got all of it, the employees none of it.

That was normal. No one questioned the justice of it. Those were the rules of the game.

But *is* it just?

It is of course perfectly fair that the founders should benefit hugely, much more than anyone else, from the value created by their ideas and initiative and risk-taking and committed work. For all her contribution, which was enormous, Greta Cameron did not create the original idea, the original business. But she made it work, and that took just about as much commitment. Without her, the original Oyster Bar might have failed; without her the first two restaurants in England might well have failed, like the first shop in Edinburgh. And if they had failed, the value eventually created would probably not have been possible.

The difference in reward for the founders and for Greta was disproportionate. The difference was created by the fact that 'ownership' of all future cash flows is not allocated to the people who create things, but to the people who provide the initial cash. It is even perfectly possible for a naïve entrepreneur to start a business and through sweating blood make it successful, and yet end up owning none of the company at all. For example, in the early days Andy Lane had given back some of his shares because Johnny Noble guaranteed at personal financial risk the extra cash needed. Johnny Noble could have played on that, could have said, 'I'm taking the risk and so I should have *all* the shares; I'll see you right when we make a profit.' Andy Lane might well have accepted that, knowing how precarious everything was. Then he would have been an employee rather than an owner – he would not have owned any part of the enormous value he helped to create.

This is not a fact of life in the sense that gravity is a fact of life. It is a human arrangement. The value created does not *have to* belong by right to the people who provide the finance. That 'right' is created by a set of contracts. It would be perfectly possible to design a set of contracts so that the people providing the cash received a limited reward and the employees shared all the rest.[14]

The argument that the creative entrepreneur should be highly rewarded is just. But it does not justify the trading of ownership rights. 'Ownership' includes the rights to all present and future profits, information and votes; they all need to be recognised as belonging properly to the people whose work creates the value (including the original entrepreneur). The current way of structuring ownership does not acknowledge the contribution of the committed employees without whom nothing could be built. It does not necessarily even recognise the rights of the entrepreneur who makes it all possible in the first place. Votes and profit – power and money – should go to the people who create value, not to the providers of the cash. Some companies move in that direction by installing share schemes for employees, usually within tight limits and using very small proportions of the shares, but only with full employee-ownership is this achieved.

It did not, of course, occur to Greta or anyone else to think like that. She was an employee. She was pleased to have the job, to be working with people she liked, to be doing things that interested and challenged and inspired her. Loch Fyne Oysters was becoming a place that people felt proud to work for. And it felt good to be needed, to have helped make it successful, to be able to do things that no one else could do as effectively. She felt lucky to have found a place where she could contribute so much. All the stuff about selling companies had nothing to do with her: that was the kind of thing that happened in Johnny Noble's and Andy Lane's world. She was just an employee, and happy to be an employee.

There was no way back on that. But now at last, after the buyout, she was an employee-owner of Loch Fyne Oysters.

18. Information

In terms of the third objective – treating all employees as real partners, fellow-owners – the first step the directors took was to provide everyone with more information. This gave the first sign that things really were different now.

Virginia Sumsion made the comparison with the old days.

> People are told so much more now. I don't think that in the past we set out not to inform people. But giving them information just wasn't part of the culture – we just didn't do it. We thought people weren't much interested but actually people are very interested. I suppose that was really poor management. But that's been a change in the culture, very much a change for the better.

The most dramatic evidence of this change in the early days after the buyout was that the venerable old non-executive chairman, Bob Craig, spent a considerable amount of time talking through the financial results with small groups of employees, eventually covering all of them. An accountant is usually the last person to be able to make numbers understandable to ordinary people, but at the very least his efforts created a recognition that this was different – the chairman really was trying to communicate. As always in developing a more participative approach, one of the most important things to achieve was to get the message across to everyone that this was for real. To do that, it was important to be seen to be genuinely trying, more important even than to get everything right. It counted for a great deal that the chairman spent time regularly giving out information, even if at first no one could understand a word of what he was saying. Of course, it was important that people eventually understood the words too, but the key thing was that they saw that the people in charge were serious about it, that this was a real change. There could not have been a more dramatic symbol of the change than to have the distinguished old chairman trying patiently, if at first with limited success, to explain the numbers to *all* the employees.

Virginia Sumsion again:

Dry financial information came out at first, but now we're explaining it in a way that makes it easier to understand. But I think we're still groping in terms of getting people to understand what the vision is for the future, what the business plan is. That's a much harder thing.

This sustained effort to communicate was hugely beneficial throughout the company – its effects probably much more far-reaching than appreciated from the vantage-point of the directors. David MacDonald, the fish filleter quoted earlier saying that he used just to come in and do his job and go home:

Now it's just so much better. I feel a lot more involved. I feel now that the higher management want lower members of staff in the production area to know more about the company. They don't hide anything. It's unbelievable how much the company's changed – it's much better, much better. I'm quite happy here now, filleting salmon every day. It's not the greatest job, but it's a job, and actually I enjoy it now because I get a lot more feedback, and I feel my work is a lot more appreciated. Everything just feels so much better.

Marby Montgomerie in the dispatch area also felt the benefits of communication.

You feel now you know a lot more. They keep you right up to date with what's going on. It feels better, because you know what's happening now, and how the company's doing.

Improving communication was thus having a direct effect on daily life. One result was that people now had a better understanding of what was going on, which in itself made a difference – it enabled them to identify with the company and to make intelligent, constructive suggestions.

But perhaps even more important, there was a change in perception about the *intentions* of 'the bosses', their attitude towards 'us' in the rank and file. The top people, however deeply respected, had been seen as fairly remote and in the end looking after their own interests; now they began to be seen as being 'on our side', and this brought a powerful positive reaction. It is worth repeating David MacDonald's delight, which was clearly triggered by his interpretation of the intentions of the managers, not simply by their actions.

> I feel now that the higher management *want lower members*
> *of staff . . . to know more* about the company. They don't
> hide anything. It's unbelievable how much the company's
> changed – it's much better, much better.

Suddenly, largely by making the overt effort to explain
what was going on, the senior managers and by extension
the whole company became more trustworthy, the whole
enterprise even more worthy of commitment. Knowing
that the company now belonged to everyone was the real
driver, in the background, but it was the behaviour of
the managers that occupied the foreground, centre stage:
clear, if occasionally faltering, proof that this was a real
change. *They care about us enough to explain things to us.*
For people accustomed and reconciled to being mere
employees, that was mind-boggling and liberating.

To the extent that this was carried forward consistently,
it began to change the nature of the institution. It began
to seem a more humane environment to work in, a place
of greater trust, more like a joint endeavour. The phrase
'carried forward consistently' was an important qualifica-
tion. Since all employees, the managers included, were
learning on the job, in the early years it was not easy to
keep it up consistently. When the pressure was on, the
old authoritarian top-down ways sometimes reappeared
and undermined the new trust. Managers sometimes fell
back on the old ways; when they did so they reinforced
the barriers of status and geography, fear of humiliation,
mistrust of motive, low self-esteem and the thousand
other little things that, as in any business, normally but
largely unintentionally kept people in their places. There
was a need for a long-term communication strategy, hav-

ing equal importance with the business strategy, and with top priority being given to its action programme. In fits and starts it began to evolve.

It may seem that all this was no more than any well-run modern business would do as a matter of course. But there was a real difference: because the company was now owned by all the employees, good communication was theirs by right, not because it would work better as a way of getting more for outside owners.

One of the constitutional arrangements aimed at facilitating communication, with the aim of achieving just such improvements, was the election of two employee-directors. On the board this was a palpable change: from soon after the buyout there were two additional people round the table at every board meeting, people chosen not for their professional skills and experience, like the sales director or finance director, but because they were trusted by their colleagues.

They brought to the board's discussions views and concerns voiced by the employees, and tried to make sure that the directors systematically communicated information – the performance, the plans, the vision, any new appointments and so on – out to everyone. Simply having them on the board provided reassurance, to all who thought about it, that nothing was being decided secretly, behind closed doors. That alone was a major change in the perception of how the company was run – it fostered confidence and trust and so prepared the ground for widespread commitment.

Being an elected employee-director was not easy on the people involved. Frances Bremner, whose job was to serve customers in the shop, was elected the year after the buyout. She was asked by a number of people to stand, not just by her colleagues in the shop, but by people who worked in production as well.

Frances Bremner had a steady look about her, a firm gaze. She had a reputation among some of the managers as being 'high-maintenance', perhaps even a bit of a troublemaker. The aspects of her character that earned her that name looked rather different from the perspective of people on the shop floor. In her own words:

> I'm not frightened to say what I think. I'm not frightened to speak up for myself or for anybody else that won't speak up for themselves.

A year later Hugh Johnston, who worked in the finance department, was similarly approached and asked to stand, by a different group of employees, including one of the directors. Sharing a car with a previous elected employee-director, he had been increasingly intrigued by hearing her talk about the board meetings.

Both Frances Bremner and Hugh Johnston felt boosted personally by the fact that people approached them. Neither of them would have had the confidence – in the west of Scotland especially it might have been seen as arrogance – to put forward his or her own name. In Hugh Johnston's words:

> It gives you a good feeling because you think people have a bit of faith in you, and think you can do the job. I was a bit hesitant actually, as I hate speaking in public, but I decided to bite the bullet. I thought it would be good for my own personal development, and I was interested to

see the workings of the company. And obviously you feel a kind of responsibility to do your best, if people are asking you to do it.

This was evident also to others in the company. Liz Long, the person whom customers speak to when they phone up to order food on the nationwide home delivery service, was delighted at what happened in the elections.

I was pleasantly surprised by the people who showed an interest in being part of the elections, either to be nominated or to nominate other people. I thought that was tremendous, the enthusiasm to get their colleagues involved, noting that this or that particular colleague would be great as an elected director. That was lovely.

And she put her finger on one reason why the sense of open communication improved as a result:

It took away the 'us and them' stigma. Initially with the first two appointments some thought, 'They're on the other side now,' but it was short-lived. People go and talk to the elected directors, which is as it should be. They may feel intimidated to speak to a higher manager or director, but to go and speak with someone they deem to be at their level is absolutely great. That's how it should be.

Both elections were contested, but there was a good spirit. Hugh Johnston again:

The person I replaced, Colin Phillips, was very gracious, and offered all his help, and we had a few chats before I

went to a board meeting. It was good hearing his point
of view rather than the other board members'.

Both of them found their first board meeting difficult.
Frances Bremner:

> It was terrifying, absolutely terrifying. I wasn't made to
> feel terrified by anyone there – it was myself, I made
> myself terrified. I'd never been to a board meeting in my
> life before so I had no idea what to expect. I was made
> very welcome and was asked my opinion on things, but
> I probably didn't voice my ideas as well as I do now. I
> thought it was a bit surreal really, me sitting there with
> the MD and all the directors. I don't think they would
> have expected much more from me, because they realised
> that I wasn't used to it.

Within a couple of meetings both said that they began
to feel confident enough to participate.

The view from the other side of the fence is also
positive, if tinged with a bit of surprise. In 2007 Bruce
Davidson, the MD who replaced Andy Lane, saw the
elected employee–director role as being difficult and
demanding, because it straddled the range of employee-
owners, from shop floor to directors. He was impressed
by how well they managed it.

> Frances and Hugh are trusted and well regarded in the
> company, because of how they have approached it. I think
> the messages they bring back are probably more believed
> than if I was bringing them. Maybe we've been particularly
> lucky, but they certainly perform extremely well.

This view was echoed by other directors, and by Virginia Sumsion, who attended the board meetings as minute secretary.

It feels very good having elected directors. I think that originally there were question marks for them, how they felt. There was a lack of understanding about what their role was. But I think the other directors have felt perfectly happy with it. They have been very welcoming and open – there hasn't been any 'them and us'.

Virginia Sumsion herself played a significant role in improving communication, producing a colourful staff newsletter regularly. Helen Seaborne, who took over as finance director in 2004, saw how important it was for the managers to keep the elected directors informed, if the beneficial effect on communication was to be sustained.

Certainly since I started there's more of an effort to make sure that Frances and now Hugh are kept informed about the day-to-day management issues. When I started we used to have regular operations meetings. Frances was left out, and it became apparent last winter that people were going to her expecting her to know things, but because she was not involved in the meetings she wasn't necessarily aware of them. But now Hugh and Frances are definitely included, not necessarily in all the operations meetings but certainly in parts of them and in the discussions on strategy and plans for the business.

At the time of writing it looked as if this aspect of the aim of having elected directors, to promote communication and trust throughout the company, was being achieved.

Each year systematic attitude surveys were carried out. The results were characteristically very positive. But the trend in the responses on communication at the time of writing is downwards. This may be because people are getting used to good communication; it may be because they are becoming more demanding, or it may be because managers have been tempted to cut corners in sustaining communication, which always absorbs time and energy. The effects are so positive, however, that the effort to sustain communication will always be worthwhile. And the employees, as owners, have the right to be informed.

19. Involvement

As well as giving out information, the managers, perhaps more tentatively, set out to listen. The human resource manager, Anne Stewart, had worked in Loch Fyne Oysters before having children. Since then she had seen in another job what happened when the company where she worked was taken over. The new owners had no interest in developing people or looking after them; they treated them uncaringly, almost as dispensable objects – an experience particularly demoralising for someone in her role. As soon as she heard about the buyout she put out feelers to see if she could rejoin Loch Fyne Oysters.

I thought the employee-buyout was a particularly good thing. What I especially liked about it was the thought that they would have to adopt a more participative style. It had been a traditional 'I say, you do', but there would have to be a change for people to feel that they had ownership. I felt that change would only be for the good.

She wanted to help shape that change, and she did. One of the early steps was to commission consultants, two women who had gained substantial experience with the Industrial Society, training people in communication. It worked well and soon the name of their consultancy, 'Lime', entered the language. 'Have you been limed yet?' people would ask if they saw someone failing to listen.

In the words of David Attwood, the operations director:

The basic thing in the Lime training was that the senior managers came together as a group of people. Rather than having walls up between the departments, we actually found out about each other. A lot of it was through osmosis, meeting and just having a cup of tea together, informal things we had never done before.

As well as encouraging the managers to get to know one another personally, the consultants used questionnaires to profile each manager psychologically. These profiles were discussed by the whole group. David Attwood again:

The startling thing was to see how different each of us is: how we tackle tasks differently and think differently and act differently, and why, as a result, any of us might have wound somebody up in the past. Particularly with the way Andy thinks: he's there already and moving on, whereas we're slowly putting each step in place as to how we want to get there. So that was very good. I think there's been good cooperation between the managers: we're in it together, doing the best we can for the company.

This was relatively standard training for managers in many businesses – it was not particular to employee-owned companies. But the logic for providing training had changed dramatically now that the company was employee-owned: it was consistent with the underlying legal rights, and not in contradiction of them. In a conventional company, there was always a fear that by providing training you were helping to make the individuals more marketable, improving their CVs with the result that they could get better jobs elsewhere and the company's investment would be wasted. Training tended therefore to be seen as a risky, costly thing and was often only grudgingly given. In Loch Fyne Oysters as an employee-owned company the idea that you should keep people less capable than they reasonably aspired to be was obvious nonsense. And anyway, why would people want to leave when they owned the company, sharing information, influence, profit and capital gain? As is generally the case, after the buyout the rate of employee turnover fell.

To the frustration of some of the managers, most suggestions put forward at first by workers were not about how to save money or how to do things better, but about issues that were pretty trivial, from a manager's point of view. There were complaints about the boots provided for those who worked in the slicing area, complaints about the changing facilities, complaints about not having a radio provided for background music.

Once those things were fixed, however, the conversations gradually changed, becoming more focused on how to do things better, how to make the business more successful. By implementing the changes on the 'trivial' issues, the managers had gained trust in the process. One day someone asked about the packaging board that was printed black on one side and gold on the other. This board was specially printed for Loch Fyne Oysters, and was expensive. The original idea, years earlier, had been to save stockholding and waste by having a dual-purpose board – using the gold side for one type of package and the black side for another. The black packaging had eventually been dropped, but through simple inertia this board continued to be ordered. One of the shop-floor workers pointed this out, and the result was a saving of several thousand pounds a year.

This was recognised as a breakthrough. That was serious money. Everyone involved realised that this kind of participation could really make a difference. For the first time the connection between ownership, involvement and prosperity was clear, not just an idea, but really working. Get everyone to play a full part, and who knows what else could be discovered, how much more saved, how much more achieved?

This was not always comfortable for the managers, even if they were drawn to the idea of the employee buyout, and even if they recognised what a big step forward it was when shop-floor employees started contributing ideas. David Attwood again:

> People now say at meetings things they wouldn't have said in the past. Before, people would just clam up and be quiet. They wouldn't raise problems with the machinery or blood-spotting on the fish, but now it comes to the surface, which is what you want. You might not want to hear it at the time [he gave a rueful laugh] but it's good for the company that you do hear it, and you tackle these problems and resolve them.

Helen Seaborne, the finance director, saw that this kind of participation would take time to mature.

> I think it's very difficult for people to understand the difference between decisions made by a manager as part

of the job of 'manager' and decisions that should be taken only after consultation with people as shareholders. There is still confusion over when you are involved as an employee and when you should be involved as a shareholder. I think it's an area that we need to keep working on.

Now that everyone was more aware of the rights that followed from ownership – although perhaps less clear about the responsibilities – this was a judgement that could trigger lively emotional reactions. Helen Seaborne:

I find it quite amazing the things that will set people off. 'Why weren't we consulted?' You can't be consulted about everything. So there is more work to be done on this.

One director found that he could not face such a change in what he saw as the proper order of things. He felt that his authority was being undermined, he didn't agree with it, and he left. The rest, however, accepted it, some even positively enjoying it. Slowly it began to seem normal.

Raymond McCaffer, the supervisor in production, was introduced by Anne Stewart to these ideas through a book, *Breaking the Mould*. It was written by an oil industry consultant, Peter A. Hunter, whose approach went much further than simple consultation, beyond the point of decisions staying in the hands of the managers. He told the story of how, by developing a sense of ownership, the workers on an oil rig deep in the Venezuelan jungle improved their performance by several orders of magnitude – reducing the time taken for a key job from eight hours to one. His first step was to call together two crews and spend an hour writing on whiteboards all their complaints, problems and suggestions about how to do it better. Having watched the meeting, the sceptical site manager summarised:

> So that's it, you just ask them how to do their job then tell them to go and do it.

Peter Hunter's comment was:

> In a nutshell, I had to admit that was what I did.
> There was however one small exception that would make the difference between the crew changing the way they worked, or continuing to work the same way they always had.
> Nobody was going to tell them to do anything.
> The crews would decide what changes they wanted to make, and then they would implement those changes themselves.

Raymond McCaffer was impressed by another idea in the book: simply providing feedback on performance in the form of numbers, not judgements or instructions, allowed people to sustain the sense of ownership. When you feel you own a company, you enjoy making it successful. So he set up a whiteboard in production.

> I'll write on the board what needs done for the day. I know how much each person can do, so I write numbers next to their names. I won't make them unachievable, I'll make them average numbers. What you find is that

most of them will surpass them. Producing 650g packs is an example. I write down '160 packs a day', and they start off maybe doing 170, they actually surpass what's expected of them already, but you see 170, 175, 180, 182 and by the end of the week they're up to about 200 packs. It does work.

He wasn't telling them what to do, nor instructing them to speed up, just giving them the numbers from time to time. They were beginning to develop a sense of ownership because of that. If it had been done in a conventional company, with the actual ownership being in the hands of outsiders, the sense of ownership would have been an illusion. It would still have felt a lot better – until the policy was changed or the managers were changed, perhaps when the company was taken over. Here, though, there was no lack of authenticity. The company belonged to them all, together, so it was absolutely appropriate to generate a sense of ownership – in fact it would have been a mistake not to. The change brought their feelings into line with reality. It was good management – stopping telling people what to do, simply allowing them to be involved, in control themselves around a common objective.

Raymond McCaffer had never had any training in how to manage. The discovery of how to allow people to perform had the effect of liberating energy and commitment in him too. When we talked he had recently asked Helen Seaborne, the finance director, for the overall numbers. In the most recent period production had been some 18 per cent up on the same period in the previous year – yet there had been two or three fewer people working in the department. But those working really were involved, in what really felt like *their* company. And it was.

20. Power and Accountability

The employee-buyout of Loch Fyne Oysters changed fundamentally the power relationships inside the company: who got to make the decisions in the company (the board rather than the founders) and the accountability (from now on the directors had to account to all the employee-shareholders for their performance, not simply to the two founders). In practice in the early period of any employee-buyout this change is not easy to make real, and Loch Fyne Oysters was no exception. At its simplest, two things were vital if democracy was to thrive: the leaders must set out to share their power, and the employees must learn to exercise theirs. More fully, those in positions of power had to give consistent, positive leadership in the direction of becoming genuinely accountable to those they led; and with the help of the leaders, those they led had to develop the understanding, confidence and initiative to enable them to play their role fully.[15]

Because Loch Fyne Oysters had only about 110 employees it would theoretically be relatively easy for the employees to supervise the directors. Between them the employees knew in detail not only what went right and what went wrong each month, but also the characters of each of the directors. They were ideally placed to make sure that any problem reached the light of day.

However, the old top-down habits had a huge

momentum behind them. There was deep respect for Andy Lane, for what he had done to build the company, and now for giving the employees the chance to own it themselves. Nobody would find it easy to stop in effect doffing the cap to him; he would face equal difficulty trying not to make the decisions himself. Habit alone, on both sides, would keep him in the position of boss, rather than reflecting the new reality, which was that the leaders of the company were now there by consent of the employee-shareholders, with authority delegated to them so that they could make decisions in the interests of everyone.

The position of chairman was by long custom similarly entrenched. Johnny Noble, like Andy Lane, had been an utterly dominant figure in the company, much loved, much laughed at and with, and not crossed or controlled by anyone. As a result, the picture of a chairman in everyone's mind was that of a commanding figure. When the new chairman, Bob Craig, stepped into the position, this traditional picture fitted well with his own instincts. His family owned the local bus company; he himself had been a naval commander; he had built up his own accountancy practice; and he had worked with small companies in trouble, where fast and effective decision-making was essential. None of this was preparation for operating in a democratic structure. Moreover, his charm, his age (seventy-three at the time of the buyout in 2003), and his obvious, energetic pride in being associated with the company had earned him the affectionate respect of a wide circle of people, who were inclined therefore to accept what he proposed and listen to his arguments without demur. He was interested in the idea of employee-ownership, and made quite strenuous efforts to communicate good information to everyone. Being accountable in any real sense, however, would be more complicated.

The employees, on the other hand, were dogged by habitual responses too, but in the other direction – the habits of those who traditionally obey rather than of those who give orders. Faced with directors who were educated, knowledgeable, and in positions of authority presumably because they had earned them, how could ordinary employees play any serious role in holding the board accountable? It was not simply that they did not feel confident, did not feel it was appropriate or within their personal capabilities and knowledge. They also carried with them the old fear: if I speak out (and it will probably come out all wrong, and perhaps sound ignorant and offensive), will the leaders not just take revenge and throw me out, or at least take it out on me in other ways?

During this initial period in any employee-buyout the progress towards a genuine, mature and successful participative partnership depends crucially on a single thing – the quality of the leadership. If the chairman and the MD understand and welcome the nature of the changes that are necessary to make the most of the new ownership structure, and if they see the opportunity for the business and for all concerned, the company will probably make the changes successfully. If, on the other hand, they are enmeshed in traditional top-down thinking and habits, and don't see sustaining the employee-ownership as a supremely worthwhile goal, the ownership will be undermined.

We have seen how the role of the elected directors had

proved effective in promoting good two-way communication. The second aspect of their role, as seen by the
people in Baxi Partnership who designed the structures,
was to deal directly with the issues of power and accountability. Constitutionally, they were supposed to solve the
problem originally posed 2400 years ago by Plato in his
Republic, and encapsulated by the Roman poet Juvenal in
his famous phrase, *Quis custodiet ipsos custodes?* 'Who will
guard the guardians?' or 'Who will govern the governors?'
In a company it is 'Who will direct the directors?' The
elected employee-directors were supposed to be the guardians of the constitution, to be prepared to speak out if
they saw something being done that treated people as if
the old system still held sway, or, worse, the directors
acting not in the interests of everyone, but in their own
personal interests.

For Baxi Partnership, the major question in designing
the constitution of Loch Fyne Oysters had been: what if
the most senior leader turns out to be either incompetent
or nefarious – a fool or a knave? If he were incompetent,
the company would be likely to fail as a business. To
protect against this, covenants were agreed so that in the
event of serious decline in the performance of Loch Fyne
Oysters it would be possible for Baxi Partnership to inter-
vene, even in extremis taking over the board.

The situation would be less clear if the leader proved
to be bad rather than incompetent. What if the MD
started pushing in a direction that would serve his own
interests, but not those of the employee-shareholders?
What if he started undermining employee-ownership
itself? Would the two elected directors on the board

enable the body politic, the employees more widely, to prevent that happening?

In theory, yes. The elected directors could tell the others what was going on, and together they could call an extraordinary general meeting to discipline or get rid of the offending MD.

And in practice? The first step would be to *recognise* what was going on. But business analyses and proposals almost never have a clear right–wrong answer – they are invariably matters of judgement. Matters of judgement are arguable. An educated and experienced business director, the sort of person who would become MD, would be good at arguing. He would also be in a position to employ consultants and advisers if necessary to build an array of convincing presentations to justify his contentions. Who among the employees would be able to take a different line convincingly, especially in the first few years?

Suppose, for example, that a bad-egg MD were approached by a large company, perhaps a customer or supplier, with an interest in acquiring Loch Fyne Oysters. If the company were to be sold, the employees would lose all their ownership rights, the rights to information, influence and wealth-sharing; the constitution would revert to a top-down structure; their working lives would relapse back to something closer to dependent servitude than shared entrepreneurship. More or less, this set of circumstances had occurred in other companies. The MD could be promised the role of MD in the larger organisation, a huge hike in salary, a considerable personal bonus. It would be easy for him to build a case. 'A larger company will have more resources to invest in us; more influence in the market. Your jobs will be more secure,' the argument would go. Temptation for the employees might take the form of the ability of everyone to sell their shares for a premium, making a short-term gain at the expense of their future working lives and those of all future generations.

The perception in Baxi Partnership was that it would be years before the understanding, confidence and procedures would effectively be in place to enable ordinary employees realistically to hold the directors accountable. For this reason, the investment agreement included the requirement for Baxi Partnership's approval of all key ownership decisions. Since Baxi Partnership was itself ruled by the trust deed set up by Philip Baxendale, requiring it to act in the interests of the employees in each company, this would form a backstop to ensure that the decisions taken in Loch Fyne Oysters would be in line with the principles of genuine employee-ownership.

In the first three years after the buyout this agreement was required over two significant issues. In 2005 Bob Craig, the chairman, proposed to transfer the ownership of the names 'Loch Fyne Oysters' and 'Loch Fyne Restaurants' to a new company, which would be jointly owned by the two companies. The idea would be to license the use of these names by other businesses, attracting income in fees and royalties that the two companies would share. The most likely licensing would be for new restaurants abroad, in which the expertise of the UK restaurant chain would be materially useful, so there was a good argument for involving them by sharing control of the brand. Moreover, most of the financing of the joint company would be done by the restaurant company, so that Loch Fyne Oysters would achieve much more active use of the brand without having to contribute any cash. This transfer would clearly make Loch Fyne Restaurants more valuable as a company – it would now be in a position of at least semi-control of its name, instead of control resting with Loch Fyne Oysters. This was a good deal all round.

It also raised the question of conflicts of interest, because Bob Craig, like Andy Lane, was a shareholder in the restaurant company. Bob Craig's expertise and his standing inside Loch Fyne Oysters meant that nobody could really question him effectively, and it fell to Baxi Partnership to raise the question of conflict of interest. Some of the directors were uneasy, feeling that following the correct professional procedure – Bob Craig and Andy Lane could contribute to the discussion, but could not vote – suggested personal mistrust. This was not at all the case, but it *felt* like disloyalty. The issue was resolved amicably and properly, and the proposal was approved, the joint company set up and the first foreign restaurant licensed, in Dubai, with the restaurant company playing a significant role in providing direction and support. The joint ownership of the brand names was put in place a few months before the refinancing of the restaurant company itself; as we have seen, the refinancing was completed successfully at a good price, which was indubitably underpinned in part by the new arrangement.

The second issue was more fraught, and took some months to resolve. It concerned the question of shares and executive rewards. Bruce Davidson, the new MD, had elsewhere been earning a salary far above the range Loch Fyne Oysters could afford. But he was relaxed about taking a lower salary if he could feel that in the event of success he would be rewarded in other ways. Bob Craig was attracted by the tax-efficiency of share options – a manager could be granted the right to buy shares at today's price, exercisable in, say, seven to ten years. So if in the interim the MD had led the company to great success, those shares would be worth much more, and he would make a considerable gain. If the share price had remained stagnant or fallen, then he would gain nothing and the company would have lost nothing. All seemingly very sensible. And in the world of management buyouts, where the ownership of shares is generally limited to the top few people, very normal.

Baxi Partnership pointed out the implications of the maths of this proposal. As previously explained, half the shares were held in trust permanently, in order to create a stable base for the ownership over the long term. This meant that only half were available for all the employees to hold directly. The constitution of the company, agreed with Baxi Partnership in the buyout, had placed a ceiling of 5 per cent on the holding of any individual. In order to allocate sufficient options to meet conventional standards for incentives, it would have been necessary to give the MD perhaps 15 per cent of all the shares. He would then have 30 per cent of the available shares, which worked out at over forty times the maximum average holding per employee. That would present no problem in a conventional company, where the employees don't count in ownership decisions, but in a company owned by all its employees, it would be seriously disproportionate.

A second aspect of the discussion was the question of who to involve in it. The previous chairman, Johnny

Noble, had enjoyed the perfect right to consult no one but Andy Lane before making decisions. The new situation was different, but the other directors, including the elected directors, were not brought into this discussion of share options until a very late stage. In a conventional company it is usual to restrict to a small 'remuneration committee' any discussion of rewards for the most senior people. This practice was initially followed more or less instinctively, even though the ownership implications of share options were fundamental for the whole company and its owners, the employees. Somehow, to those involved it did not seem right for elected people to be discussing the MD's reward package – the reality of the new situation did not yet seem natural.

The question: 'Who's boss around here anyway?' also seemed to hover in the background from time to time, and to play a part in the tension that developed for a period between Loch Fyne Oysters and Baxi Partnership. At root the point under discussion was a policy matter: 'What is the greatest proportion of the shares that any one person should be permitted to hold in a company owned by all its employees?' This should have been resolved by rational discussion and agreement. But it looked to me as if the chairman resented what he appeared to see as unwarranted interference by Baxi Partnership in a decision that seemed to him self-evident, and which, given his standing and the rudimentary stage of democratic development in the early years, he could easily persuade others to agree to. At one point Bob Craig declared that he would lead a bid to take over Loch Fyne Oysters, because he believed that by doing so he could force Baxi Partnership out. He admitted to us in Baxi

Partnership that the real driver for him was the question of the options – he wanted to raise the ceiling for the MD to much more than 5 per cent of the shares. If they bought the company, they would be free to do so. In doing so he still wanted, he said, to preserve the employee-ownership. In our view it was likely that the result of any such buyout would be much closer to a normal MBO, with ownership concentrated in the hands of a few senior people, rather than all-employee ownership with genuine involvement and accountability to the employees. Moreover, a future sale of the company would be almost inevitable, ending the rights of the employees. This, of course, was in our eyes a direct contradiction of Philip Baxendale's vision – strong companies, in all-employee ownership, with partnership cultures – which we were duty bound to implement, as well as being personally inspired by.

None of this was a case of nefarious conspiracy – simply confusion caused by the conflict between on the one hand the need to sustain genuine all-employee ownership and, on the other, ideas that seemed self-evident coming from a background of conventional ownership structures and the skewed share-ownership and top-down decision-making structures that flow from them. Nonetheless, significant dangers for all-employee ownership arise when people who have a great deal of power are caught in conventional models of ownership, while those around them are unaccustomed to having any influence at all.

In the end a compromise was reached, with an agreement to pay Bruce Davidson substantial cash bonuses over the long term if performance improved, and also to raise his shareholding ceiling to 10 per cent – everyone was delighted that he wanted to buy a significant proportion of Andy Lane's remaining shares, and a 10 per cent ceiling enabled him to do so. This would give him about twenty-five times the maximum average holding of the other employees.

One result of this process was the realization that it was asking a lot of the two elected employee-directors to carry out the supervisory role – they were outnumbered on a board dominated by professional directors, a board which was constantly dealing with commercial matters that were often outside their areas of competence. Another outcome was an agreement to work towards Loch Fyne Oysters flying free from Baxi Partnership. The two were linked: before agreeing to the removal of the 'backstop' provisions, Baxi Partnership would have to satisfy their trustees that in any new arrangement Loch Fyne Oysters would be likely to sustain their business success, their all-employee ownership and a genuine partnership approach to management. An essential requirement would be that the supervisory elements of the constitution were strengthened, and that people at every level had a good understanding of them, and the confidence and motivation to make them work.

It seemed to all concerned that the trustees of the Loch Fyne Oysters trust were the obvious candidates to take on a greater supervisory role. They owned 50 per cent of all the shares, and held them solely in the interests of all the employees. Quite naturally, this gave them real constitutional power, and the legal duty to behave in a principled manner. In law, trustees' duties were sometimes narrowly interpreted as being to look after the purely financial interests of their beneficiaries; in the case of Loch Fyne Oysters the trust deed had been written to give them the right to consider the broader interests of the employees, and of the future employees as well. As a result, the trustees were enabled to take into account the fact that the employees benefited from being employee-owners, and would continue to benefit if the system was maintained; if the system ended, for example by the sale of the company, it was clear that future employees would not benefit at all, either financially or in the wider sense of being in charge together of their own company.

At the time of writing, there are three trustees elected by all the employees, and one professional lawyer. Ideas are under discussion for increasing the number of elected trustees, and embedding their role more firmly in the governance of the company. In this way it is intended both to ensure that they are fully representative of public opinion within the company, from top to bottom, and also that they have the influence to act as guardians of the constitution, with the board reporting to them regularly. It is the trust that is the very embodiment of the fact that everyone together owns the company, everyone together makes it successful and everyone together shares in the rewards of doing so. The intention is that these privileges will be sustained and passed on to future generations. In the end, what happens will be up to the people there at the time, and whether they continue to act competently, energetically and in good faith towards sustaining the all-employee ownership and the democratic, partnership approach.

The AGM held in November 2007 was from this viewpoint a little disappointing to some. The attendance was large – over half the employees – but down on previous years. For the first time, Andy Lane was not present – he came off the board from the date of the meeting. Bob Craig gave a short talk about the previous year and plans for the future. He was heard with serious attentiveness, but there was no real questioning of him or the board. Then, with formal ceremony, the necessary resolutions were put to the meeting. On the way in, slips of paper had been handed to individuals, telling them to propose or to second a particular motion – that hardly felt like the flowering of democracy. It was the turn of Bob Craig to step down as a director, and, appetite undiminished at the age of seventy-seven, he was putting himself forward for re-election. For that part of the meeting he handed the chair over to Simon Briggs, the sales director, and left the room.

General meetings are potentially important occasions for making clearly visible the reality that the board is accountable to the employees. John Lewis do this quarterly: the directors in turn are cross-examined by a council of over 100 elected people, and the exchanges are published verbatim in the weekly *Gazette*. At Tullis Russell's AGM there are presentations by the MD, the finance director and sometimes division leaders, as well as a report from one of the elected representatives on the Share Council. Then the whole board sits in front of the meeting to answer questions, an interrogation which can take more than an hour, before the formal business is taken. In Loch Fyne Oysters, as this book goes to press, the reality of accountability has yet to be made manifest. That development will depend on the instincts and appetites of the leaders, and the active initiative of employees.

21. How Are They Doing?

The full effect of the employee buyout of Loch Fyne Oysters will only be seen over many years. People take time to grasp the opportunities provided by change, particularly fundamental change.

At the time of writing, late 2007, the signs are positive – LFO is thriving as an employee-owned company.

Since the buyout, the company has faced a number of threats, as all companies do, small companies perhaps more starkly than others because their resources are less substantial. For example, in 2003 the British Airways first-class menu proudly included Loch Fyne Oysters' smoked salmon, and Loch Fyne Oysters were even more proud to have it there. A few months after the buyout, however, the SARS virus threatened the world with an epidemic. International travel fell drastically, and British Airways saw a dramatic reduction in ticket sales, particularly in the Far East. Already in the throes of retrenchment following the effects on air travel of 9/11 and the Iraq War, the airline saw its credit rating downgraded by one agency specifically due to the additional SARS-related fall. Sales of salmon to British Airways dropped significantly. Since they could only be replaced by sales to others of less high-margin products, the profits of Loch Fyne Oysters suffered collateral damage.

Another significant risk is the price of salmon: raw salmon is the largest single purchase made by Loch Fyne

Oysters, and its price tends to fluctuate dramatically. In
the late 1970s they had started by buying all their salmon
from the fishery that netted wild salmon at Inveraray, a
few miles along the coast. But that fishery had seen the
salmon stocks collapse, partly due to overfishing at sea,
and partly due to the ruin, through forestry, of good small
salmon rivers, each of which had started with its own
unique salmon population returning annually. Forestry
drainage filled the streams with fine sand, which blanketed
the redds – the gravel spawning beds – and also damaged
the fish's gills. In the case of the Kinglas River, silt blocked
up the dam and filled in the pool where the salmon had
previously waited for the spates. The close-packed trees
in the artificial forests created perpetual shadow, dis-
rupting the plant and insect life; they also constantly
dropped large quantities of pine needles, rendering the
water too acid for eggs to develop. Finally, the forests
were sprayed with pesticides, with the result that the rivers
and even areas of the seabed at their mouths were rendered
barren.

For this reason Loch Fyne Oysters had early on made
a stand against smoking and selling wild salmon, until
the stocks recovered. Instead, they worked with specific
salmon farms approved by Andy Lane. In 1999 they
appointed as their main supplier the salmon farm at Loch
Duart, a model of nature-friendly fish farming. In Loch
Duart far fewer salmon were accommodated in each cage,
and a system was in place which left each cage lying
fallow every third year so that the parasites did not get
established, making it unnecessary to use polluting chemicals in the water. At the time this meant that Loch Fyne
Oysters had to pay £2.90 per kilo as opposed to the

prevailing market price of £2.20. It was a high price to pay for sustainability – but it was worth it to walk their then still unfashionable talk, and particularly so when the taste came through, and they started winning blind tastings. The market price of salmon continued to fluctuate, and after the buyout reached an extraordinary peak in 2006: £3.60 per kilo, an increase of 50 per cent over the price of less than £2.40 in July 2003. Again, profits suffered, and again, the benefits of the increased productivity that tend to accompany employee-ownership came into their own: more throughput with less waste made Loch Fyne Oysters better able to survive this peak in costs.

Overall, the result was that sales grew in every year after the buyout, adding over 50 per cent in four years to reach £11.5m, greatly helped by the ever-growing demand from the expanding chain of Loch Fyne Restaurants. But profits fluctuated from year to year, with a low point of £430,000 in the year of the buyout, and a high of £630,000 in the following year. The high was not sustained, partly because to achieve the sales growth thinner margins had to be accepted on some business, partly because of the cost of salmon, and partly because of building capability and making investments to grow the business and provide better service.

From these operating profits they had to pay the interest on the borrowings taken on to fund the buyout itself, so the reported profit after interest was significantly lower after the buyout – less than half of the £550,000 achieved in the year before it. Nonetheless, a growing overall trend was established, the borrowings began to be repaid, and as mentioned before, enough leeway was generated to pay a dividend in 2006, very popular with the employee-owners.

As this book goes to press in late 2007 it seems that the three aims expressed in Philip Baxendale's vision are being achieved: Loch Fyne Oysters is indeed a strong business, it is certainly in employee-ownership, and with increasing understanding and appetite, the beginnings of a real partnership culture are in place. Less than five years is a short time for such a profound change in culture to bed down, but Loch Fyne Oysters is well on the way.

Epilogue
A Dream Fulfilled

Let me take you back briefly to June 2005, to a conference crammed with about 100 people from employee-owned companies. Andy Lane moves forward to speak – his slot in the programme has arrived.

He looks tall and slightly awkward, balding, gangly in his customary dark blue fisherman's jersey, his eyes hidden behind spectacles. He shifts from side to side, saying nothing. The audience quietens, and the hush becomes intense, expectant, even slightly worried – has he forgotten what he is going to say?

At conferences like these, gatherings mainly of practitioners and believers, the people in the audience are in search of stories that will inspire them and reinforce their beliefs, and of ideas that they will be able to take away and use in their own working lives, to do things better. The presenters are generally experienced in the field, and with developing technology the standard of presentations is high, if a little uniform in style.

This conference is about employee-ownership. Nothing jars the consensus: employee-ownership is a good thing.

Andy Lane's manner when he starts to speak is diffident, quiet, almost mumbling.

I haven't got a presentation, so I brought you this picture instead.

The screen changes to a huge panorama of Loch Fyne. The waters of the sea loch are sparkling deep blue under a hot sun, the air so clear across the mountains that you fancy not a mouse could move without attracting attention. It is days like these that make Highlanders glad of the rain and storms, the cold and the midges, which combine to keep the visitors down to reasonable numbers. If it were too often like the picture on the screen, the place would be overrun.

A long pause. In the audience there is an outbreak of shifting and squirming. Andy Lane has their attention, but is this going to be a disaster? He looks a bit odd – does he know what he's up to?

Finally:

I'm in a war, in the trenches,

His voice is quiet.

Bullets are flying all over the place.

There is a gap after each sentence. It really seems that he is not sure what he is going to say next.

A spent bullet falls at my feet, and I pick it up.

Pause.

On the bullet some words are engraved.

Utter quiet. People crane forward.

'Made by the Acme Bullet Company'.

And, after another brief pause.

'Employee-owned'.

The tension relaxes, one or two people give snorts of laughter. But this is not what is expected. Does Andy Lane believe in employee-ownership or not?

With the same slow delivery, he describes how a second bullet thumps into the wall of the trench, and he picks it up. This one is also made by the Acme Bullet Company, employee-owned. Something else is written on it: Fair Trade.

He continues, speaking more strongly now:

Employee-ownership is great. It has saved the soul of the company we built, and it is good for everyone working in it. It is the right way to own a business. But it is not enough. You have to choose what kind of business you are going to be in. Employee-ownership does not make it OK to make money by killing people or by trashing the planet.

He goes on to explain that employee-ownership makes a business more efficient, but it might simply make an immoral business more efficient at being immoral. Without ethical principles things can go badly wrong. Using examples from the area of Loch Fyne, he charts the depletion of natural resources over 150 years, the destruction of the huge herring shoals, the disastrous effect on the local communities, the near-impossibility of arresting similar declines.

Loch Fyne Oysters, he tells the audience, has worked from the first in ways designed to turn that round. Its produce is sustainable, naturally pure. The move to employee-ownership is perhaps the final element, making it a totally ethical company. It is now a force for regeneration of natural resources and of the local community. As he finishes, the audience applauds with more than politeness.

I am reminded of what he said as he was reflecting on the strains of the early days.

> We were seen as nutters for years. This was never going to work; it was a joke. We weren't taken seriously. Which was fine, because in some ways it's nice to be unconventional. But as we've become successful we've drawn more into the mainstream. That does give you more influence: you can start to change the world around you.

Nearly half a century earlier, he had sworn he would devote his life to looking after wild things, looking after nature. Now he has passed into the ownership of all its employees a business that does just that. The eight-year-old has fulfilled his vow.

Furthermore, those coming after him are picking it up. Liz Long, who liaises with the home-delivery customers from all over the UK, expresses how it feels to work in Loch Fyne Oysters.

> I feel comfortable. I'm happy in my work, and I feel safe. And I feel safe for the community as well, which I think is important.

Responding to the suggestion that for employees to have such feelings would be anathema to City financiers, who would predict a decline in performance as a result, she gives off sparks.

Yes, I'm sure they would say that. But for me it's the opposite. You can't be complacent – that would be wrong, and we would quite rightly be criticised. We're not complacent at all, we realise that we need to work hard to survive and to keep going. It can only be done with hard work. I would fight tooth and nail to keep us successful here.

She clearly means it. Commitment is strong stuff.
David Attwood, the operations director, reflects on what makes Loch Fyne Oysters special.

The location, the area, Ardkinglas House, the loch, the hills, the glens. Then what we're dealing with: oysters, luxury seafood, locally sourced for sustainability. The people, working together, looking after each other, looking after people's careers, homes, families. Care of the environment, the sea: how dependent we are on it – our products need clean seas. Leaving clean seas for our children. Looking after things, recycling, treating our planet with respect. All these things are woven into it really, and it makes it quite a special business to be involved with. I'm very proud of the company I work for. To be able to say that I'm a director of Loch Fyne Oysters gives me immense pride.

Acknowledgements

I have been hugely helped by many people, to whom I am deeply grateful. Many at and around Loch Fyne Oysters subjected themselves to hours of interrogation, and checked that I had reported correctly what they had said. Their names are in the text. Andy Lane – who offered support tirelessly at every stage – and Liz Lane and Virginia Sumsion read the whole thing at an early stage, and Christina Noble most of it, all giving invaluable corrections and feedback. Isobel Dixon made an enormous contribution: she suggested I write the book in the first place, and proved an enthusiastic, supportive and resolute agent. John Alexander cheerfully took over my role at Baxi Partnership, giving me time to write. Hugh Andrew proposed the title *Local Heroes*; he and Dan Hind provided early feedback and encouragement. Judy Moir believed in the book from when it was only half written, and has been the most perceptive and illuminating of editors. In the process of copy-editing, Helen Campbell also greatly improved the clarity and flow. Jenny Dean shaped the later stages with skill and enthusiasm. David Ellerman developed many of the key ideas reflected in my thinking. Chris Mackin found J. S. Mill's 697th paragraph, used as an epithet. My wife Jennie's painstaking edits saved me from much embarrassment; she has been, throughout, supportive beyond the call of duty, and a walking contradiction of the Japanese *Senryu*, 'When you happen upon your wife in town, it isn't stimulating.'

Between them, they are responsible for anything good. Any remaining dross is mine alone.

David Erdal
January 2008

Further Reading

1. Books and Papers on Employee-ownership and Employee Share Ownership

Blasi, Joseph, Douglas Kruse and Aaron Bernstein, 2002. *In the Company of Owners: The truth about stock options and why every employee should have them*. New York: Basic Books. A look at stock options, which can trigger some – but not all – of the beneficial aspects of employee-ownership.

Bradley, Keith, and Simon Taylor, 1992. *Business Performance in the Retail Sector*. London: Clarendon. These two economists established that over the seventeen years measured, both the capital productivity and the labour productivity of John Lewis were the highest in the retail trade.

Broad, Gayle, and Linda Savory-Gordon, 2006. 'Worker ownership as a strategy for community development', in Eric Shragge and Michael Toye (eds), *Community Economic Development: Building for social change*. Sydney, Nova Scotia, Canada: Cape Breton University Press. Two academic researchers discuss how the wider benefits of employee-ownership can help build communities.

Conyon, Martin, and Richard Freeman, 2001. *Shared Modes of Compensation and Firm Performance: UK evidence*. NBER (National Bureau of Economic Research) Working Paper No. 8448. A study by two authoritative economists of the link between productivity and employee-share schemes in

300 quoted companies in the UK. The regressions showed a large effect, and that the all-employee scheme had approximately 50 per cent greater impact than the scheme giving options only to senior managers.

Ellerman, David, 1992. *Property and Contract in Economics: The case for economic democracy.* Cambridge, Mass: Blackwell. eText available from www.ellerman.org/Davids-Stuff/AboutDavidEllerman.htm

Ellerman, David, 2005. '*Translatio* versus *Concessio*: Retrieving the debate about contracts of alienation with an application to today's employment contract'. *Politics and Society*, 33: 449–80. eText available from www.ellerman.org/Davids-Stuff/AboutDavidEllerman.htm

Ellerman, David, 2006. 'Three Themes about Democratic Enterprises: Capital structure, education and spinoffs'. eText available from www.ellerman.org/Davids-Stuff/AboutDavidEllerman.htm. David Ellerman has long been one of the seminal minds working on employee-ownership.

Freeman, Richard, Douglas Kruse and Joseph Blasi, forthcoming 2008. *The Economics of Shared Capitalism.* New York: Sage. This book by three pre-eminent researchers in the field is eagerly awaited.

Gates, Jeff, 1998. *The Ownership Solution.* London: Allen Lane. A book that fizzes with ideas for how employee-ownership can be developed and used. Gates was counsel to the Senate Finance Committee, which established the first legislation favouring employee share ownership in the United States.

Hoe, Susanna, 1978. *The Man Who Gave His Company Away: A biography of Ernest Bader, founder of the Scott Bader Commonwealth.* London: Heinemann. A biography of one of the colourful pioneers of employee-ownership in the UK.

Law, Andy, 1998. *Open Minds: 21st century business lessons and innovations from St Luke's*. London: Orion. The cracking tale of the employee-buyout of the London advertising agency and their radical approach to democratic management.

Lewis, John Spedan, 1954. *Fairer Shares: A possible advance in civilization and perhaps the only alternative to communism*. London: Staples Press. This book sets out in a unique style the philosophy of the founder of the John Lewis Partnership.

NCEO (National Center for Employee Ownership), 2004. *Employee Ownership and Corporate Performance*. California: NCEO www.nceo.org/pubs/corporateperformance.html. The NCEO is the key source in the United States of good-quality information on employee-ownership.

Oakeshott, Robert, 1978. *The Case for Workers' Co-operatives*. London: Routledge & Kegan Paul. Oakeshott started as a foreign correspondent of the *Financial Times*, and switched in the 1970s to being one of the first and best advocates for employee-ownership in the UK.

Oakeshott, Robert, 2000. *Jobs and Fairness: The logic and experience of employee ownership*. Norwich: Michael Russell. An authoritative book of UK, European and American case studies, and discussion of their implications.

Savory-Gordon, Linda, 2003. 'Spillover effects of increased workplace democracy at Algoma Steel on personal, family and community life'. PhD thesis, University of Bristol, Faculty of Social Sciences, School for Policy Studies. Seminal research showing how, after an employee-buyout, skills learned through playing a greater part at work were transferred and used in the community.

Whyte, William Foote, and Kathleen King Whyte, 1991. *Making Mondragon: The growth and dynamics of the worker cooperative complex*. Ithaca: Cornell University Press. An authoritative work on the group of over 100 worker-cooperatives in the Basque region of Spain, employing over 70,000 people, with their own bank, university and social security system.

2. Books and Papers on Wider Subjects Tangential to Employee-ownership

Bruner, Robert F., 2005. *Deals from Hell*. New York: John Wiley & Sons. A detailed analysis of ten significant corporate mergers that failed.

Daly, Martin, Margo Wilson and Shawn Vasdev, 2001. 'Income inequality and homicide rates in Canada and the United States'. *Canadian Journal of Criminology*, vol. 43: 219–36. This study confirmed that homicide rates are higher where inequality is greater, also testing and rejecting competing explanations of the data.

Frank, Robert, 1988. *Passions Within Reason: The strategic role of the emotions*. New York: W. W. Norton. An economist applies games theory and evolutionary insights to psychology, with interesting results, particularly on the subject of commitment.

Johnston, M., V. Morrison, R. MacWalter and C. Partridge, 1999. 'Perceived control, coping and recovery from disability following stroke'. *Psychology and Health*, 14: 181–92. An important paper on health, establishing the beneficial impact of seeing oneself as in control.

Kelly, Marjorie, 2001. *The Divine Right of Capital: Dethroning the corporate aristocracy*. San Francisco: Berrett-Koehler. A well-written critique of corporate power and capital markets in America.

Marmot, Michael, 2004. *Status Syndrome: How your social standing directly affects your health and life expectancy*. London: Bloomsbury. A lucid discussion, for the general reader, of the fact that people lower in social standing die younger. Marmot is one of today's great epidemiologists, unusually capable of writing clearly and simply.

Mill, John Stuart, 1909 [1848]. *Principles of Political Economy with some of Their Applications to Social Philosophy*. London: Longmans. The full text is available at <u>www.econlib.org/ Library/Mill/mlPContents.html</u>. Part II, chapter VII, paragraphs 697 (used as an epigraph) and 736 predict the development of employee-ownership, and some of its beneficial effects.

O'Sullivan, Mary, 2000. *Contests for Corporate Control: Corporate governance and economic performance in the United States and Germany*. Oxford: Oxford University Press. This powerful critique shows how emphasising shareholder value fails to foster the innovation that is the real creator of wealth.

Wilkinson, Richard G., 2005. *The Impact of Inequality: How to make sick societies healthier*. London: Routledge. One of the key, highly readable, texts on the relationship between health and inequality, by one of the originators of the field.

Notes

Full publication details for works cited here will be found in Further Reading.

1. See Robert F. Bruner (2005), *Deals from Hell*.
2. See Keith Bradley and Simon Taylor (1992), *Business Performance in the Retail Sector*.
3. There is a large literature, mainly from US data, on the effects of employee-ownership. A good survey is found in the National Center for Employee Ownership (2004), *Employee Ownership and Corporate Performance*. The most up to date will be the forthcoming book edited by three pre-eminent researchers in the field, Richard Freeman, Douglas Kruse and Joseph Blasi (2008), *The Economics of Shared Capitalism*.
4. The 'spillover' effects of the Algoma Steel employee-buyout were studied by Linda Savory-Gordon, for her unpublished PhD thesis (2003). See also Gayle Broad and Linda Savory-Gordon (2006), 'Worker ownership as a strategy for community development'.
5. See for example the paper written by the team led by Professor Marie Johnston of Aberdeen University: M. Johnston, V. Morrison, R. MacWalter, C. Partridge (1999). 'Perceived control, coping and recovery from disability following stroke'.
6. See Marmot (2004), *Status Syndrome: how your social standing*

directly affects your health and life expectancy, written for the general reader by the outstanding researcher in the field, Sir Michael Marmot.

7. See Richard G. Wilkinson (2005), *The Impact of Inequality: How to make sick societies healthier.* Professor Richard Wilkinson is one of the originators of this field.

8. See for example Martin Daly, Margo Wilson and Shawn Vasdev (2001), 'Income inequality and homicide rates in Canada and the United States'.

9. Even in Scandinavia wealth is becoming more polarised. e.g. 'Few countries have more equal income distribution . . . [but s]ocial polarisation and segregation by income . . . has increased in Scandinavian cities since the early 1980s. Hard numbers in the form of Gini coefficients . . . reveal this trend.' Hans Thor Andersen and Eric Clark (2003), 'Does the welfare state matter? Ghettoisation and the welfare state'. In Jan Ohman and Kirsten Simonsen (eds), *Voices from the North: New trends in Nordic human geography.* London: Ashgate, pp. 91–106

10. By far the most wide-ranging and insightful survey of employee-owned companies both in the UK and internationally is Robert Oakeshott's (2000) book of case studies and discussion, *Jobs and Fairness: the logic and experience of employee ownership.*

11. See note 1. For a superb and rigorous exposition of how real wealth is built through committed investment and innovation rather than by stock markets or by corporate expansion through acquisitions, see Mary O'Sullivan (2000), *Contests for Corporate Control: Corporate governance and economic performance in the United States and Germany.*

12. See Robert Frank (1988), *Passions Within Reason: The*

strategic role of the emotions, an amusing and insightful book. The passage on the scepticism of behavioural scientists (including economists) is on pp. 20–21.

13. Martin Conyon of the University of Chicago and Professor Richard Freeman of Harvard and the London School of Economics analysed UK data on quoted companies. They showed that all-employee share schemes are associated with a particularly strong effect on productivity. See Conyon and Freeman (2001), *Shared Modes of Compensation and Firm Performance: UK evidence.*

14. This analysis owes a great deal to the work carried out over decades by Professor David Ellerman, formerly senior economist and advisor to two chief economists of the World Bank: Joseph Stiglitz, 1997–9, and Nicholas Stern, 2000–3. Ellerman (1992), *Property and Contract in Economics: The case for economic democracy,* was a turning point for me. There is a useful summary of the main arguments in his 2005 paper, '*Translatio* versus *Concessio*: Retrieving the debate about contracts of alienation with an application to today's employment contract'. His 2006 paper, 'Three themes about democratic enterprises: Capital structure, education and spinoffs' extends and clarifies his arguments. Both the book and the papers are available free on his website. www.ellerman.org/Davids-Stuff/AboutDavidEllerman.htm

15. Don José María Arizmendiarrieta, the inspirational founder in the 1950s of the Spanish Basque grouping of over 100 employee-owned companies centred on the town of Mondragon (under whose name it is known), encapsulated this point as follows: 'Our beloved democracy may degenerate into a dictatorship through the abuse of power by those at the top, as well as through the renunciation of power by

those at the bottom.' Mondragon, in 2007 employing over 70,000 people, provides strong evidence to counter those who are pessimistic about the practicality of business success in employee-ownership. For the story of Mondragon, see Oakeshott (2000) and Whyte and Whyte (1991).